PHILOSOPHY, HISTORY AND POLITICS

MELBOURNE INTERNATIONAL PHILOSOPHY SERIES

VOLUME I

PHILOSOPHY, HISTORY AND POLITICS

NATHAN ROTENSTREICH

Communications to be addressed to the Editor, c/o Philosophy Department, University of Melbourne, Parkville, 3052, Victoria, Australia.

Philosophy, History and Politics

STUDIES IN CONTEMPORARY ENGLISH PHILOSOPHY OF HISTORY

by

NATHAN ROTENSTREICH

MARTINUS NIJHOFF – THE HAGUE – 1976

PRINTED IN THE NETHERLANDS

AUTHOR'S NOTE

The present book selected some theories in contemporary English philosophy whose pivotal points are the relations between the activity of
philosophy, the realm of history and the political concern. The author
has attempted a balance between description, analysis and criticism.

Jerusalem, 1973   N.R.

TABLE OF CONTENTS

CHAPTER I

THE SHADOW OF HISTORY OVER PHILOSOPHY: R. G. COLLINGWOOD

A. FACTS AND THOUGHTS

I

There is a common distinction between two aspects of history: history as the object dealt with and history as the way of dealing with the object. Within the "objective" aspect of history one may distinguish between the attempt to define the object as man and the attempt to define it as process. Within the "subjective" aspect there is the prevailing tendency to put forward the nature of the method as one employing individual concepts.

In spite of the many-sided development it underwent, Collingwood's view of the nature of history can hardly be classified in accordance with these distinctions. Though he dealt with the two aspects of history mentioned above, Collingwood did not draw a precise distinction between them. In the first step he made as a systematic thinker, Collingwood attempted to define the nature of history through the nature of the historical object. But since the consideration of the nature was included from the outset in *Speculum Mentis*, which is, and perhaps was meant to be, a kind of "Phenomenology of Spirit", he could hardly ignore the problem of knowledge and its relation to the nature of the object. Let us therefore consider how he approached this problem in the first period of his development.

"History is that which actually exists."[1] "The object of history is fact as such."[2] Obviously this approach tends to define the nature of history by stating what historical knowledge has necessarily as its object, namely fact. History is not defined as a branch of knowledge dealing with a fact in *time*, nor as dealing with the facts of *human* life, etc. It is just an attachment to fact, that is considered the essence of history. Even the fact that historical knowledge deals with the past

[1] *Religion and Philosophy*, London, 1916, p. 49.
[2] *Speculum Mentis*, Oxford, 1924, p. 211.

is not derived from any particular relationship between this knowledge and time in its dimensions. The nature of a fact is, according to Collingwood, a sufficient guide in determining the relation between history and the past: "the historian's business is with fact; and there are not future facts."[3] The aspect of time is obviously secondary in this view. It is an outcome of the nature of facts and not an independent factor.

A further characteristic feature of the nature of the historical object *qua* a fact is its individuality. Nothing new is added through this feature, since "matter of fact" and "individuality" might be considered as synonymous. Collingwood does not determine the meaning of "individuality" at this point, e.g., whether or not the historical fact occurs only once; and it is not clear whether this is the meaning he attached to individuality, since this meaning carries with it from the outset the aspect of time, which is not the aspect stressed by Collingwood in the first place. Individuality connotes a matter of fact, that is to say, the impossibility of deducing the fact from a hypothesis or from a systematic setting. Once we assume deducibility, the deduced element ceases to be individual and becomes a variable in a set of replaceable elements. A fact is bound to be individual, since we are bound to accept it as it is, precisely because it is given.

The relationship between individuality and historical knowledge has been discussed extensively in modern philosophy. The purpose of this discussion – in which Collingwood also participated – was to point to the nature of the historical method and its conceptual apparatus. Collingwood does not regard individuality as a feature of this apparatus, but as the nature of the object itself. He assumes that the nature of the object guides historical knowledge in employing conceptual ways and means to square with the object.

The cognitive attitude adequate to the object as fact is *assertion*. Assertion suggests the acceptance of the object as it is, and because it is. An assertion is a categorical statement, i.e. the admission that something exists as something concrete and given. Historical knowledge as assertive is opposed to scientific knowledge as hypothetical. In a way, Collingwood arrives here at a paradoxical conclusion: historical knowledge, being related at its objective pole to facts and at its subjective pole to assertion, must be a naïve knowledge, a receptive one. This conclusion may be an indication of Collingwood's form of idealism in his early period. Constructions, as manifested in science, are – according to Collingwood – a lower stage in the development of the forms of

[3] *Ibid.*, p. 217.

mind and reality than assertions of the given concreteness. Once we reach the stage of concreteness there is no legitimate room for constructions. Constructions indicate the gap between the knowing subject and the known object and therefore they are bound to remain abstract. Once we reach a meaningful reality we have but to recognize it as such, that is to say, to assert it. It goes without saying that this systematic presupposition of Collingwood's view blocked the way towards an analytic understanding of the nature of historical knowledge. The very fact that Collingwood eliminates hypothetical statements from history and confines historical statements to assertions, indicates that he does not do justice to historical reasoning: every historical inference is hypothetical, running from given data to their causes. As a passage from data to their causes historical inference is hypothetical and there is no room here for mere assertion of causes. It is clear, in terms of the history of ideas, that Collingwood wanted to transgress the boundaries of historical knowledge as outlined by Bradley; but he did not succeed in doing so.

The consideration of history as related to facts on the one hand, and to the assertive act on the other, led Collingwood to a paradoxical historical conclusion. Philosophy of history as manifested in Vico was explicitly anti-Cartesian. Descartes has been blamed for being abstract; hence philosophical prominence has been given to history as a concrete creation. Collinwogod, although rooted in the Viconian tradition, considered the main achievement of Descartes to be precisely in the discovery of history. "Descartes, in his *cogito ergo sum*, laid down that historical fact was the absolute meaning of knowledge."[4] Only because Collingwood gives history a generic meaning as knowledge of ultimate-irreducible facts, can he identify historicity with the objective of Descartes. In his view, "*cogito ergo sum*" expresses a fact; hence the nature of Descartes' statement is a historical one. Here Collingwood's tendency becomes clear: history deals with facts; hence where one finds an attitude of *hypotheses non fingo*, there one finds history. Indirectly Collingwood meets here the criticism of the Cartesian tradition as expressed in Vico. According to Collingwood, Descartes does not assume a self-sustained abstract knowledge. "Descartes meant what he said; and what he said was that the concrete historical fact, the fact of my actual present awareness, was the root of science. ... Science presupposes history and can never go behind history: that is the discovery of which Descartes' formula is the deepest and most fruitful expression."[5] Vico, on this

---

[4] *Ibid.*, p. 199.
[5] *Ibid.*, p. 202.

view, did not realize the concrete, historical-factual basis of the Cartesian abstraction.

The structure of the Cartesian system is an example of the nature of the dependence of science upon history and a further means of clarifying the nature of history. If history employs assertions and is categorical, science employs suppositions and is hypothetical. Collingwood tried to show that each supposition presupposes at least one assertion, the assertion that there is supposition here. In other words, science as a texture of suppositions presupposes history as a body of assertions. The logic of Collingwood's conception of the relation between science and history can be summed up in two points: (1) There is no possibility of an infinite regression of suppositions. The end of the claim of suppositions implies an assertion of fact. (2) Thus a chain of suppositions ultimately leads to facts, and this is the domain of history. Science implicitly presupposes history, while the realm of history proper is the explicit manifestation of the implicit presupposition. In this period of his development, Collingwood tried to overcome the duality of science and history through a dialectical device: he made the two realms into stages in the manifestation of Mind, giving each of them its relative justification. This dialectical justification of the various stages of development of Mind was possible on the basis of the underlying assumption, that is to say that the difference between the stages is one of *modality* of assertions and not one of *material* content or *ontological* realm. "The abstract cannot rest upon the more abstract, but only on the concrete,"[6] and history is the first acknowledgement of concreteness.

At this stage, the elimination of any construction in history led Collingwood to the assumption of an inner relation between the historical attitude and philosophical realism. "Fact is something independent of my own or your knowledge of it."[7] "The historical form of dogmatism is that represented by modern realism ... which results from discovering the concept of fact."[8] This is one of the most remarkable traits in the whole of Collingwood's development: since it rests on the very assertion of given facts, history is thought to be connected with epistemological realism. It is precisely here that the fundamental change occurred in the later stage of Collingwood's thought: history will then be connected with an anti-realistic attitude, as against the realism expounded by the "minute philosophers". But this change was made pos-

[6] *Ibid.*, p. 185.
[7] *Religion and Philosophy*, p. 49.
[8] *Speculum Mentis*, p. 281.

sible only by a change in Collingwood's entire philosophical attitude. In the period of *Speculum Mentis* Collingwood employs a clear-cut dichotomy: hypothesis on the one hand and assertion on the other. Assertion was considered to be characteristic of a higher cognitive level than hypothesis. The entire system, including the relation of history to philosophy, is based on this primary assumption. This dichotomy, in turn, was based on the consideration of concreteness as the ideal goal of knowledge, parallel to the consideration of concreteness as the ultimate stage of the manifestation of Mind. One may say that here the Hegelian attitude becomes apparent, as the knowing subject becomes submerged in the object; the view of epistemology itself is a sign of the gap between subject and object, a gap which must be overcome. Once concreteness is the ideal, there is no room for cognitive *activity* on the part of the subject. As against this dichotomy in the early stage, another dichotomy is put forward in the mature stage of Collingwood's system, that of *questioning* against *assertion*. With this new dichotomy a new understanding of history emerges in Collingwood's system.

This clinging to the given facts is the first point to be stressed in terms of the limitations of history as a form of Mind. The very possibility that history may lead to a dogmatic attitude indicates the weakness of history. Dogmatism is rooted in the assertion of something as ultimate, though in reality it is only provisional. Historical knowledge assumes that what is asserted as a fact is a real fact; it does not recognize its own immanent limitations. It considers its own facts to be recognized as given and hence as the real facts. But these facts cannot be real since they are set in a partial context only. Facts included in an all-embracing context, Collingwood therefore argued, are facts known by philosophy and not by history. The aim of history is to know the facts, but it does not reach this goal because the context is always partial and thus incomplete. If we do not know the complete context, we do not even know the single fact, according to the Hegelian maxim that the truth is the whole. "If history exists, its object is an infinite whole which is unknowable and renders all its parts unknowable." "As long as we pretend to write history we must claim access to the fact as it really was. This fact . . . is inaccessible. History as a form of knowledge cannot exist."[9] Historical knowledge condemns the knowing subject to a passive position of sheer assertion. In the last resort there is no meaningful room within the historical domain, as the domain of an assertion of facts, for the status of the knowing subject. If, however,

[9] *Ibid.*, pp. 234, 238.

the subject is eliminated, there could be no justification of the claim of historical knowledge to be a knowledge of the concrete. There is only one legitimate meaning of the notion of concreteness, that of totality. But totality is outside the scope of historical knowledge. Totality as the all-embracing context is a philosophical concept and not a historical one. Thus history is only on the threshold of philosophy, since it intends to reach concreteness but does not reach it. Philosophy requires the victory of history over science[10] since it presupposes the establishment of the striving towards concreteness. But philosophy ultimately overcomes history, just as an objective arrived at overcomes the sheer striving for it and the formulation of it. History ends with its own breakdown; but this is a positive, i.e. a dialectical breakdown, since out of the debris of history philosophy emerges.

In an earlier book, Collingwood had formulated the relation between history and philosophy as one of identity which later on became a *Leitmotiv* of Collingwood's system: "History *a parte objecti* – the reality which historical research seeks to know – is nothing else than the totality of existence; and this is also the object of philosophy. History *a parte subjecti* – the activity of the historian – is investigation of all that has happened and is happening; and this is philosophy too. History and Philosophy are therefore the same thing."[11] This emphasis on the identity of the two realms does not reappear in *Speculum Mentis*, but we may perhaps see the difference in the attitudes between *Religion and Philosophy* (1916) and *Speculum Mentis* (1923) as a difference in point of view only, and not as a fundamental one: the claim of history is to be philosophy. This claim ,however, does not succeed, because of the immanent limitation of history as the knowledge of given facts. *Religion and Philosophy* stresses the identity of history and philosophy in terms of the programme, while *Speculum Mentis* stresses the difference between the two realms in terms of the *realization* of the common programme. In both works the intermediary between history and philosophy is the striving towards concreteness, which in turn implies totality. The connection of history with the aspect of totality and concreteness did not leave room for the plane of time. On the contrary: since concrete totality is self-contained, the problem had to be raised whether or not time is included in the all-embracing totality. According to Collingwood, history does not deal with data in time, but with data as such. Hence the problem of the relation between data and time has not been raised.

---

[10] Cf., *ibid.*, p. 246.
[11] *Religion and Philosophy*, p. 51.

But the time aspect appears in *Speculum Mentis* indirectly, though it does not fit organically into the entire conception as outlined in this book. The aspect of time appears in connection with the problem of novelty in history on the one hand, and of permanence on the other.

It is a process in which method or regularity does not exclude novelty; for every phase, while it grows out of the preceding phase, sums it up in the immediacy of its own being and thereby sums up implicitly the whole of previous history. Every such summation is a new act, and history consists of this perpetual summation of itself.[12]

Here at once the aspect of process comes to the fore, although this aspect had not been stressed when the nature of history was considered in terms of its status in the chain of manifestations of Mind. It goes without saying that there is no point in considering the aspect of novelty and summation unless we presuppose the background of time. But the relation of history to time remains a riddle in Collingwood's system in all its phases and is one of the paradoxes of his entire conception. Collingwood aims to consider history *sub specie aeternitatis* and thus expel, as it were, time from history. He was so eager to stress the identity of history with philosophy that he tried to abstract history from its real milieu and to deal with history without dealing with time. This is like Hamlet without the Prince of Denmark.[13]

2.

The conception of history as outlined in *Speculum Mentis* underwent several fundamental changes. Between the earlier and the later conception there is an intermediate one, expounded in a paper of 1925 where Collingwood emphasized not so much the *factuality* of history as the *individuality* of historical events. Yet this might be regarded as a change in terminology only, a change which has some basis in Collingwood's explicit criticism of history, since he tries now to show that history is in the end an unachievable task: "The alleged facts upon which history builds its inductions are actually never secure enough to bear the weight that is put on them."[14] Collingwood criticized history in *Speculum Mentis* as being pretentious, as attempting to reach totality which is beyond its

---

[12] *Speculum Mentis*, p. 56.

[13] The status of time in Collingwood's system has to be dealt with separately. See the present author's *Between Past and Present, An Essay on History*. New Haven, Conn., 1958. See also the subsequent chapters.

[14] "The Nature and Aims of a Philosophy of History", *Proceedings of the Aristotelian Society*, Vol. XXV, London, 1924–1925, p. 152.

power. There was no question as to facts, and therefore Descartes'
"*cogito*" as an isolated fact or a statement of a fact was not put in
doubt. To be sure, no fact could be understood unless placed in the
context of totality, and this context was thought to be set by philosophy
and not by history. The question could be raised in the context of
Speculum Mentis whether a fact can be considered as being a fact when
isolated from its context, or whether we may still assume the existence
of the fact and stress the importance of the context only for the understanding of its full meaning. The realistic trend involved in history
would refer to the independent *existence* of the given fact, while a full
understanding of the fact would necessarily overstep the scope of the
fact as such. The paper of 1925 marks possibly the emergence of his
understanding of the relation between the two aspects of history. Facts
are no longer considered as confined to themselves apart from their
being understood: "inductive study is itself based on ascertained facts,
but these facts in their turn can never at any given moment finally be
ascertained, for instance the discovery of this Roman villa may bring
into question doctrines hitherto generally accepted as to the provenance
and date of some kinds of pottery."[15] Here Collingwood explicitly accepts the standard of "the truth as the whole" as the inner standard of
history. Yet this standard eventually shows the limitations of historical knowledge. Collingwood no longer distinguishes between the fact
as such, which is ascertained in its givenness, and the meaning of the
fact, which places the fact in a context. He assumes only one legitimate
context – that of totality. Actually, the historical fact, even when placed
in the total context, does not lose its individuality; it might be for this
reason that at this stage of his doctrine Collingwood stressed the trait
of individuality in the nature of the historical object more than the
trait of factuality.

The cognitive act which characterized history in *Speculum Mentis*
was assertion. In the paper of 1925 Collingwood, writing of the act of
perception, presents it as an activity on the part of the knowing subject. He stresses the aspect of activity in perception by putting to the
fore the *judgment* implied in perception: "in all perceptions we are
making a judgment, trying to answer the question what it is that we
perceive, and all history is simply a more intense and sustained attempt
to answer the same question."[16] Collingwood criticizes the dichotomy
of sensation and thought, with the view to showing that sensation itself

[15] *Ibid.*, p. 153.
[16] *Ibid.*, p. 168.

involves an act of thought.[17] If sensation implies thought, then perception also implies thought in its shaped form as judgment. The aspect of
judgment in perception is revealed through an important notion, which
occupies a central position in Collingwood's later system. Even perception, he argues, is an act of answering a question. The x is not sensed
as such. Perception interprets the x and determines its nature and
meaning, and this determination is certainly an activity. "History is
perception raised to its highest power, just as art is imagination raised
to its highest power."[18] Thus from two points of view the former conception of history undergoes a far-reaching change. From the point of
view of the object, factuality ceases to be understood in a naïve way
as something merely given. From the point of view of the subject, historical knowledge is no longer mere assertion; it is perception and as
such a manifestation of a cognitive activity. These two angles of criticism are interrelated: since the fact is not given, it is in a way created,
through the act of perception. The object of history is not defined as
independent of the knowledge of it, "the historian's data consist of
what he is able to perceive."[19]

The criticism of the shortcomings of historical thought as outlined
in the system of *Speculum Mentis* was based on the assumption that
historical thought does not establish the total context. One of the
expressions of the partialness of the historical context was the fact that
the historian is himself left outside the context of his thought. The gulf
between object and subject was an indication of the inherent weakness
of history in its unrealizable pretention to be concrete. This criticism
is re-stated in the article on "The Nature and Aims of a Philosophy of
History," but the context of the criticism is different now. The relation
between history and philosophy is no longer that of the formulation of a
programme and the fulfilment of it. History is "object-centred" thinking, it "asks questions only about its own object, not about the way in
which it comes to know that object."[20] The fact that the historian is
not included in the setting of his thought is an outcome of the very
trend of historical thought. This trend may be stated as follows: historical thought is a *perceptive* thought but not a *reflective* one. The historian is "always the spectator of a life in which he does not participate:
he sees the world of fact, as it were, across a gulf which, as an historian,

---

[17] See "Sensation and Thought", *Proceedings of the Aristotelian Society*, Vol. XXIV, London, 1923–1924, pp. 55–76.
[18] "The Nature and Aims of a Philosophy of History", p. 167.
[19] *Ibid.*, p. 170.
[20] *Ibid.*, p. 164.

he cannot bridge.''[21] Here, again, the shift in Collingwood's understanding of history becomes clear: history is finite not only because its
subject-matter is partial and, as partial, can be never definite. It is finite
because the subject or the knower remains on a plane different from
that of his object. The finitude of history lies in the very duality of
subject and object. To put it in other words: within the system of
Speculum Mentis factuality was regarded as an advantage of history as
against the hypothetical nature of science, which is based on a chain
of suppositions. The problem of the gap between subject and object
was hinted at, but it was only a secondary feature related to incompleteness of history. In terms of assertion on the part of the knower
there was no room to point to the gulf between the knower and his
object. Once the active nature of the subject has been brought to the
fore, the whole perspective changed: in perception considered as judgment, or act of thought, the knower is separated from his object.
Against the totality of facts, objectively considered, a new totality is
hinted at, comprising both subject and object. In both works, the main
concept in Collingwood's understanding of history is that of totality.
In *Speculum Mentis*, history had a realistic feature. Totality was realistic at least in its claim: a totality of facts placed on an all-embracing
context of facts. In the paper of 1925, a new aspect of history comes to
the fore: history as an activity of thought. Totality, here, is understood
as containing both the subject and his object. The relation between
history and philosophy in *Speculum Mentis* is one of a programme and
its fulfilment, while the relation between history and philosophy in the
paper of 1925 is one between naïve thought, which is object-centred,
and reflective thought. Reflective thought is understood in terms of
Hegel's conception of self-consciousness as an identity of subject and
object.

The change in the meaning of totality might be tied up with the
change in the whole systematic approach. *Speculum Mentis* is – as said
before – a kind of Phenomenology of Spirit in the Hegelian sense, a study
in the progressive manifestations of Mind or Spirit. History is one of
the forms of Spirit: it is Spirit as it manifests itself in actuality. The later
phases of Collingwood's philosophy were at least more modest – or to
put it differently – not phenomenological in Hegel's sense, but epistemological. History is no longer understood as a manifestation of Spirit, but
as a form of knowledge. Philosophy of history is mainly a theory of
historical knowledge and not a theory of the status of history in the

[21] *Ibid.*, p. 165.

progressive manifestations of Spirit. Therefore the problem of totality arises within the scope of historical consciousness and not within the scope of historical facts. From this point of view the article of 1925 is at least an anticipation of the new approach as it was to be formulated in the mature system.

3.

Collingwood's view of the nature of history still changed in the course of time. There is in the first place an assumption which might be considered trivial when detached from the earlier view, or from the far-reaching conclusion derived from it in the mature view: history is "knowledge of the world of human affairs."[22] The neutral object of history as fact becomes now a specific object within the human realm.

What is the background of this new understanding of the nature of history? Collingwood himself seems to give us a clue to the hidden motives which led him towards this change. In the first place, the deeper understanding of the nature of fact accomplishes the first change. '"Facts 'is a name for what history is about: *facta*, *gesta*, things done, πεπραγμένα, deeds."[23] Here Collingwood still refers to the first meaning of the term "facts" which indicates their givenness. But "facts" has also a secondary sense, πεποιημένα "things made". "A making is a deed; a thing made is the result of a deed. To know about deeds is to know about their results ..."[24] And: "The results of deeds are abstractions from the deeds; the historical method involves studying both deeds and their results: in this case, both mental activities and their results, for example concepts."[25] There is a kind of regress carried out from facts *qua* results to the process creating them. Historical method is interested both in the results and in their background. In dealing with historical facts *qua* results, Collingwood performs a reduction from facts to motives. History does not deal with facts as events; it deals with events as actions – the term action is intended to connote both the aspect of motive and that of results. Since the historical concern has been placed in the human realm, the historical fact which was in the first place the ultimate datum ceases to be ultimate. It necessarily points to its background within the human realm, to motives, thoughts and purposes expressing themselves in acts. For the sake of convenience we may call

---

[22] *An Autobiography*, Penguin Books, 1944, p, 79.
[23] *The New Leviathan*, Oxford, 1942, p. 61.
[24] *Ibid.*, p. 61.
[25] *Ibid.*,

this new view the anthropological view of history. There emerges now the new conception which explicitly does not identify events with historical objects: "I mean more than he (sc. S. Alexander) does by the word 'historicity'. For him to say that the world is a 'world of events' is to say 'the world and everything in it is historical.' For me, the two things are not at all the same."[26]

This shift to the human realm carries with it a new understanding of the individuality of the historical object. There is no longer an attribution of individuality to a neutral object; individualtity has now a *human* meaning. It connotes a human being whose deeds are understood in terms of historical method. In its shift from events to thoughts history studies individuals. Individuality ceases to be a mark of the given object, or else a conceptual device, and is held to reside in the very nature of the specific object of the research. Yet this confinement of individuality to the human sphere is the source of a new problem in Collingwood's system. Since the historical individual expresses himself in thoughts which in turn lead to results, individuality cannot be "monadic." "Because individuality is the vehicle of a thought which, because it was actually theirs, is potentially everyone's."[27] We have to point out that this change undermines the clear connection of history with individuality, which was so much stressed in the former view. The individual nature of the historical object is itself a fact. But there is no essential connection between the object of history *qua* thought or purpose and the individual who personally was the bearer of the thought. The connection between the real object of history *qua* actions rooted in thoughts and the human individuals in whom these actions actually did occur, is accidental. Indeed, Collingwood comes back here to the Hegelian conception of the "cunning of Reason," and views individuals as embodiments and agents of the Reason of history. Individuals cease to be considered as ultimate self-sufficient entities.

A further significant change occurred in the shift from knowledge based solely on the ascertaining of facts to a knowledge based on questioning. In Collingwood's approach to history there is an increasing of activity *"a parte subjecti"*; from an assertion which indicates the sole acceptance of the fact, he moved to perception which contains the activity of judgement; from this he moves further to the "Baconian understanding of history," viz. to the challenge of the given circumstances by putting questions to them. The difference is stressed in the

[26] *The Idea of History*, Edited by T. M. Knox, Oxford, 1945, p. 210, note.
[27] *Ibid.*, p. 303.

following passage: "The questioning activity, as I called it, was not an activity of achieving a compresence with, or apprehension of something; it was not preliminary to the act of knowing, it was one half, the other half being answering the question of an act which in its totality was knowing."[28]

4.

The "Baconian" approach to history points to the purposive nature of history, while the purposive nature of the historical actions makes the questioning activity possible, and altogether meaningful. There is thus, in Collingwood's mature system a double contraction of the realm of thought. History proper, in Collingwood's view, becomes history of *thought*. Thought is not understood as mere content or meaning, but receives from the outset a connotation which is intended to make it suitable for the historical context: thought is *purpose*, either purpose as the driving force of an action, or purpose as the end the action is aiming at. Thought is understood as intentionality towards the future and as moving towards it. The purpose of historical understanding is to discover from the results the action which created those results. "Political theory is the history of political thought: not 'political theory,' but the thought which occupies the mind of a man engaged in political work: the formation of a policy, the planning of means to execute it, the attempts to carry it into effect, the discovery that others are hostile to it."[29] This example taken from the field of political history is a clue to the whole of Collingwood's later system of historical knowledge: Collingwood could place history in the realm of purposive activities since in the later phase of his development he did not take into account the objective circumstances in which the purposive activity takes place, for instance, the geographical data essential for purposive planning of an action, or the stamina and endurance of a people or a society which is called upon to act, etc. Collingwood – and this is the main criticism of his view with reference to his contraction of history to purposive activities – placed the activity, as it were, in a vacuum; he understood it as having meaning only when related from the outset to meaningful activity. The only meaningful activity which he took into account was that of sponsoring an action with a purpose in view. But in history there are meanings assigned to given facts through responses to circumstances:

[28] *An Autobiography*, p. 22.
[29] *Ibid.*, p. 75.

an earthquake, although by no means a purposive activity created within the human realm, has a historical meaning through its impact on the human realm, that is to say through the meaning connected with this disaster after the event and not in anticipation of it. This is another indication of Collingwood's anthropological view of history: man is a being who projects the future, a being to whom the future is not given but rather who creates it through his own deeds. Hence history as an understanding of human affairs has to discover this essential feature of human existence. Collingwood, however, detached human activity from its given environment and took into account only the meanings created by a purposive action and those anticipating the forthcoming results.

Historical research, however, does not deal with thoughts within the realm of one's own life. Thought creates results, and unless it does so it is inaccessible to the historian. The first condition for a historical object *qua* thought to be known is the expression of thought in the realm of facts. Collingwood remains faithful to his original understanding of the nature of the historical object *qua* fact, but goes beyond the realm of mere facts by rooting them in the realm of thought. This is the first condition which makes historical knowledge possible *"a parte objecti."* But there is another condition, *"a parte subjecti"*: "the historian must be able to think over again for himself the thought whose expression he is trying to interpret."[30] What kind of condition is brought to the fore in this formulation? The first condition is an epistemological one: unless it has results, there is no way of knowing the thought itself. The second condition, that *"a parte subjecti,"* sounds like a psychological one: one has to be a mathematician, at least a potential one, in order to understand mathematics, or one has to be able to reconstruct the plan of a political action in order to understand a historical political action. This condition has been provided for in the very fact that historical knowledge deals with thought, and thought is not confined to the individual existence since it has a universal meaning. Furthermore, the fact that history deals with thoughts makes it *a priori* understandable for a historian. The condition formulated concerning the ability of the historian to re-think the investigated thought sounds like a condition stated for a philologist to be able to read the script of the text he is dealing with.

There is a clear epistemological advantage implied in this shift towards thought. There is no room for a sheer ascertaining of thoughts, as if they were meaningless facts. Since we move in the realm of meaning,

---

[30] *Ibid.*, p. 76.

the ascertaining of the fact of thought is *eo ipso* an understanding of it. "To *discover* that thought is already to understand it. After the historian has ascertained the facts, there is no further process of inquiring into their causes. When he knows what happened, he already knows why it happened."[31] The ontological nature of the historical realm *qua* thoughts leads to some clear epistemological consequences: toward thoughts there is only one possible attitude, that of a thoughtful activity. "*A parte subjecti*" this activity means understanding of the motives and purposes expressed in deeds. To *know* a thought means to *understand* it.

Collingwood had expressed this view in an earlier article: "What happens, happens for a good reason, and it is the business of history to trace the reason and to state it. And that means to justify the event."[32] This line in Collingwood's thought can be understood in the light of his later development: since every historical act is an outcome of a purposive action, every act is understandable and as understandable it is justifiable. Justification does not mean approval of the act but detection of its motives. Collingwood rejects explicitly the moral approval of every act, once we understand it in its motive: "... this truth is grossly distorted if it is twisted into the service of a vulgar optimism which takes it for the whole truth."[33] The half truth hinted at refers to the feature of the understanding as an *intellectual* act and not as *moral* approval. It seems to regard that the nature of historical knowledge as the understanding of a thought does not lead to the Leibnizian optimism, which Collingwood rejects, but rather to a tolerance, the nature of which he formulated in connection with Ruskin's view as 'the activity to live one's own life and yet to admire and to love people who live by the systems which one rejects.'[34]

We have considered what Collingwood understood as the second condition of historical consciousness, i.e. the mind of the historian. This condition has been regarded as trivial, since it puts forward the psychological disposition of the historian and not the objective character of historical consciousnesss. Collingwood would reject this interpretation because of the subjectivist trend of his new system. History shifts, in his view, from the domain of the understanding of the specific nature of the object to the emphasis on the meeting between object and sub-

---

[31] *The Idea of History*, p. 214.
[32] "Croce's Philosophy of History", *The Hibbert Journal*, Vol. XIX, p. 274. Compare *Speculum Mentis*, p. 218.
[33] *Ibid.*
[34] *Ruskin's Philosophy*, London, 1920, p. 20.

ject. This is a subjectivist interpretation of the saying, "*Die Weltge-schichte ist das Weltgericht.*" In the Hegelian context this saying pointed to the trial within the actual historical process, where the superseding events determine the success and the value of the previous events. Collingwood put into this saying a new content: "*Die Weltgeschichte ist das Weltgericht:* and it is true, but in a sense not always recognized. It is the historian himself who stands at the bar of judgment, and there reveals his own mind in its strength and weakness, its virtues and its vices."[35] How could Collingwood attribute to the old saying this subjectivist connotation? The starting-point of Collingwood's new understanding of history lies in the assumption that all history is the history of thought. Thus history is, of necessity, from the outset a meaningful realm. This is a kind of axiomatic assumption of his entire view. If so, then it is the task of the historian to detect the meaning of the realm he is investigating. If he fails in that, his failure is an indication of his own weakness, and not of the absence of meaning in the events as such. As a matter of principle, the historical events as such are understandable since they are events in the realm of thought. The failure to understand them is henceforth a psychological or spiritual weakness on the part of man who tries to understand them. This is a mitigated version of the former trend: although historical events are not justified, they are understandable. Again the spiritual nature of history comes to the fore: within the system of *Speculum Mentis* it was inherent in the status of history as one of the forms of Mind, although Mind manifested itself in neutral, *prima facie* non-spiritual, phenomena of facts. Within the later system, the spiritual nature of history appears in the very content of the historical object.

However, there remains the question of how Collingwood could attribute this fundamental status to the strength or to the weakness of the historian's mind. If historical events are meaningful in themselves because they are placed within the domain of thought, how can the historian fail to understand them? "The historical process is itself a process of thought, and it exists only in so far as the minds which are parts of it know themselves for parts of it." If the mind of the historian is a part of the process, then how is it that *it* stands at the bar of judgment and not the mind which exhibits itself in the events investigated? Either the mind of the historian has an independent standing and thus there is no self-evident identity between history as *res gestae* and their nar-

---

[35] *The Idea of History*, p. 219. For a different interpretation of the saying see *Speculum Mentis*, p. 218.

ration, or else it is a part of the historical realm. Hence there cannot be a problem of principle connected with the mind of the historian, which is fundamentally a part of the objective realm.

5.

There is a lack of symmetry in Collingwood's theory of history, because the status of the historian's mind is by no means as essential as the status of the object of his mind as thought. But Collingwood, for systematic reasons, wanted to emphasize the parallel status of the historical object and the historical subject. He even made this parallelism the main point in his criticism of the approach to history of the German school on the one hand, and that of the contemporary French philosophical school on the other:

Whereas the German movement tries to find the historical process objectively existing outside the thinker's mind, and fails to find it there just because it is not outside, the French movement tries to find it existing subjectively inside the thinker's mind, and fails to find it because, being thus enclosed within the subjectivity of the thinker, it ceases to be a process of knowledge and becomes a process of immediate experience: it becomes a merely psychological process, a process of sensations, feelings, and sentiments. The root of the error in both cases is the same. The subjective and the objective are regarded as two different things, heterogeneous in their essence, however intimately related. This conception ... is wrong in the case of history, where the process of historical thought is homogeneous with the process of history itself, both being processes of thought.[36]

The error of both schools lies in their one-sidedness; only Croce, as Collingwood observes, grasped the synthetic nature of history. But Collingwood is actually closer to the German school than he himself was aware of: although he tries to establish the synthesis between thought as object and the mind of the historian, the mind of the historian has only a secondary status, since the meaningful event is bound to be understood precisely because it is meaningful. The mind of the historian may have values as an example of the height human understaning is able to reach, but according to the principles of Collingwood's own view it cannot have an ontological status. Although Collingwood strove in his later conception of history towards a well-balanced synthesis of object and subject, he still retained a conception which attributes a preponderance to the historical object.[37]

[36] *Ibid.*, p. 190.
[37] There is growing literature on Collingwood. Consult *Critical Essays on the Philosophy of R. G. Collingwood*, Edited by Michael Krausz, Oxford, 1972, pp. 327ff. (contains Collingwood's Bibliography).

B. HISTORY AND PHILOSOPHY

I.

Having considered several different conceptions of the character of historical thinking in Collingwood's system, we may now examine the question, What status does history occupy in relation to philosophy? Since this question is among the central themes in Collingwood's system, his attempts to cope with it can serve as a suitable point of departure for the present part of our exploration.

To begin with, it should be observed that the entire texture of Collingwood's system is historical, history constituting both its implicit background and one of its explicit components. Before turning to examine the explicit historical element in his system, it would be pertinent to consider the implicit historical background against which it developed.

As already observed, in *Speculum Mentis* Collingwood expounds a kind of Phenomenology of Spirit along genuinely Hegelian lines. Three elements of Hegel's *Phenomenology of Spirit* interact in Collingwood's "Phenomenology," namely: (a) an analysis of consciousness; (b) an analysis of the historical development of the various activities in which Spirit manifests itself; and (c) an analysis of the various manifestations or forms of Spirit.

Collingwood's "Phenomenology" differs from the Phenomenology of Hegel in the strong emphasis it places on the historical character of the very problem which demands a synoptic or systematic approach to the diverse forms of mind. According to Collingwood, "art, religion, and philosophy are not really the same thing: there are differences between them which need not appear as long as they are at a comparatively low level of development, but appear all too sharply when they reach maturity."[1] In other words, only when the interrelated domains of

[1] *Speculum Mentis*, p. 29.

Spirit manifest the full diversity of their content does there arise a
problem concerning the systematic structure of the diverse manifestations or forms of Spirit. The emergence or appearance of these forms
is an historical fact which came into being in a specific historical situation pervaded by a specific climate of opinion. Tracing the emergence
of the diverse forms of Spirit to the Renaissance, Collingwood maintains
that "freedom, the watchword of the Renaissance, meant freedom for
all the different activities of the mind from interference by each
other."[2] In other words, he believes that the specific circumstances
which created the specific cultural setting of the Renaissance, liber-
ated the diverse realms of experience, or the diverse realms of mind,
from the intermingled relationships in which they had hitherto been
enmeshed. The appearance of each spiritual form, in its full essence,
dates from the Renaissance. From that time on, the relation among the
diverse, semi-independent domains has presented a problem. Thus,
the problem of a system of human experience arises only with the
emergence of a plurality of diverse realms of experience. Before the
problem can present itself, the plurality of domains must make itself
manifest in a particular historical situation.

By this Collingwood obviously does not mean to imply that the
specific historical circumstances which prevailed during the Renaissance created the problem of a system of human experience. The problem is inherent in the very essence of mind. What he means to imply
is only that the systematic problem is made manifest by a particular
historical situation. History constitutes the background against which
the manifestations of mind emerge, as well as one manifestation of
mind among others. This brings us to a question which Collingwood
himself did not cope with in a satisfactory manner. What he did not
clarify was the double position which history occupies in his system as
(a) the background against which all the realms of mind are made
manifest; and as (b) one of the five realms (art, religion, science,
history and philosophy) encompassed by the domain of mind. Thus
one factor in Collingwood's system which contributed to its pervasively
historical texture consists in the double role played by history: (a) as a
spiritual form in its own right and (b) as the background against which
all spiritual forms are made manifest. Because Collingwood himself
does not clarify the double meaning of history,[3] the inner relation between the two meanings remains an unsolved problem.

[2] *Ibid.*, p. 30.
[3] History occupies the same dual position in Cassirer's *Philosophy of Symbolic Forms*. Compare the present writer's "Cassirer's Philosophy of Symbolic Forms and the Problem of History", *Theoria*, Vol. XVIII/1–2, 1952, pp. 155–173.

Another factor in Collingwood's system which renders its texture pervasively historical consists in the correspondence which he posits between the diverse spiritual realms and the successive stages of mankind's development. According to him, "childhood, adolescence, and maturity seem . . . to correspond with art, religion, and science as their proper spiritual antitypes,"[4] and "the same general tendency towards a series of phases beginning with art seems to be at work in the history of mankind."[5] Thus, besides manifesting their independence of one another in a specific historical situation, the diverse forms of mind also constitute a series of successive phases in the history of humanity. The dialectical-conceptual process whereby one form – owing to its dialectical-conceptual shortcomings – is superseded by another form, accordingly corresponds to the actual and factual process of historical events. In this respect, Collingwood may be said to combine his basically Hegelian approach with a Comtian trend. His Comtian treatment of the phases of mankind's development brings into prominence both the historical background of the diverse forms and the historical texture of his entire system.

2.

Collingwood maintains that once the forms do manifest their partial independence of one another, there arises the problem of the system of forms. It is in that context that the question of the relation between history and philosophy arises. Although Collingwood himself does not call attention to it, there is a significant parallelism between the positions occupied by history and philosophy respectively in the system of the diverse spiritual forms. Just as history is at once one form among others and the background against which all the forms manifest themselves, so philosophy is at once one form among others and the all-embracing systematic framework in which all the forms are absorbed. As the *background* of forms, history is parallel to philosophy as the *totality* of forms. In history the diverse forms of spirit are embedded implicitly, whereas in philosophy they are absorbed explicitly.

But whereas history fulfills a twofold function in relation to the other forms of mind, philosophy fulfills a threefold function in relation to them. The first function of philosophy *qua* totality is to define the nature of each form in itself and the nature of the relation which obtains

---

[4] *Speculum Mentis*, p. 51.
[5] *Ibid.*

among the diverse forms. To put it another way, the first task of philosophy – once the diverse forms have made their independence of one another manifest – is to survey all of them synoptically and to place them in their proper position on the map of mind. The second function of philosophy, which follows from the first, is to justify the diverse forms of mind by elucidating and rendering explicit their essence and their place in the totality. The third function of philosophy is to criticize the forms precisely by allotting to each its proper place. Each form, in other words, purports to be *the* totality. By circumscribing the position of each form on the map of mind, and by revealing its inherent limitations, philosophy criticizes all the forms and exposes – to paraphrase Whitehead's expression – the fallacy of "misplaced completeness" inherent in their claim to totality. Accordingly, the third task of philosophy is to show that the stubborn resistance offered by each form to the verdict of incompleteness passed upon it, is dogmatic. For, as Collingwood points out, "dogmatism is simply the resistance which a given form of experience presents to its own destruction by an inner dialectic."[6] Hence, the function of philosophy is to reveal that the diverse forms are "philosophical errors."[7]

Yet it is not only by defining their limits and exposing their limitations that philosophy criticizes the diverse forms of experience. It also criticizes them by exposing what might be called the antinomy or the gap between their latent spiritual essence and their manifest concrete appearance. "In art, religion, science and history," Collingwood argues, "the true object is always the mind itself: it is only the ostensible object that is other than the mind."[8] The only form of mind which no longer involves a gap between inner essence and outer appearance is – philosophy. In philosophy mind is at home; for here its essence is realized in a conceptual totality.

This conception of philosophy as the form most consonant with the essence of mind is a further reflection of Collingwood's debt to Hegel. What distinguishes Collingwood's approach from that of Hegel is, *inter alia*, the fact that he adds science and history to Hegel's list of spiritual forms which had originally included only art, religion and philosophy. Unlike Hegel, Collingwood regards history not only as a background process of mind, but also as a form. Hence, unlike Hegel,

---

[6] *Ibid.*, p. 259.
[7] *Ibid.*, p. 250.
[8] *Ibid.*, p. 249.

Collingwood is confronted with the problem of the relation between history and philosophy.

3.

It has already been pointed out that the problem of the relation between history and philosophy constitutes one of the central themes in Collingwood's thought. It may now be added that in the course of his development, Collingwood suggested several different solutions to this problem. Having seen how the problem is presented by the trend of Collingwood's thought, whose texture is pervasively historical, it remains to see how he attempted to cope with it.

Collingwood's initial conception of the relation between history and philosophy is suggested by his statement that history cannot exist without philosophy.

> There is no such thing as an entirely non-philosophical history. History cannot proceed without philosophical pre-suppositions of a highly complex nature. It deals with evidence and therefore makes epistemological assumptions as to the value of evidence; it describes the actions of historical characters in terms whose meaning is fixed by ethical thought; it has continually to determine what events are possible and what are not possible, and this can only be done in virtue of some general metaphysical conclusions.[9]

This statement suggests that the relation between history and philosophy is not one of *identity* but one of *inherence*. Philosophy is inherent in three aspects of history: its epistemological assumptions, its ethical criteria, and its metaphysical conclusions.

This conception of the relation between philosophy and history is clearly too narrow. For it is not only history that is based upon philosophical presuppositions and subject to philosophical criteria. Philosophical assumptions and criteria are operative in all forms of cognitive activity whose method is scientific. By its very nature, the use of scientific method involves conformity to epistemological criteria such as those associated with the problems of the datum, verification, the relation between empirical and rational factors, etc. Thus, to take an obvious example, an epistemological (and consequently, philosophical) problem is inherent in the question – causality or statistics – raised by modern physics. Thus the dependence upon philosophy is not an exclusive characteristic of history.

Having posited the dependence of history on philosophy, Colling-

---

[9] *Religion and Philosophy*, p. 46.

wood advances a step further, and posits the dependence of philosophy on history. "Philosophy," he writes, "is impossible without history. For any theory must be a theory of facts, and if there were no facts there would be no occasion for theory."[10] To understand this statement, it is necessary to notice, (a) that Collingwood uses the term "theory" as a synonym for "philosophy"; and (b) that he is recapitulating, briefly, a view concerning the categorical nature of philosophy which he had expounded in detail in his *Essay on Philosophical Method*. In that work he had argued that philosophy formulates conceptual statements about reality or about facts, which statements imply the existence of the objects corresponding to the concepts under consideration.[11] At this stage in the development of his thought, Collingwood maintains that by virtue of its concern with facts history approximates philosophy, which is likewise an intellectual activity concerned with facts. From his conception of the relation between history and philosophy as one of *inherence*, he has accordingly advanced to a conception of this relation as one of *proximity*.

Apparently dissatisfied with the notion of *proximity*, Collingwood attempted to establish the *identity* of history and philosophy. His argument in support of this identification reads as follows:

History – "*a parte objecti*" – the reality which historical research seeks to know – is nothing else than the totality of existence; and this is also the object of philosophy. History – "*a parte subjecti*" – the activity of the historian, is investigation of all that has happened and is happening, and this is philosophy too. History and philosophy are therefore the same thing.[12]

It is worth mentioning in passing that Collingwood's tendency to identify history and philosophy reflects the strong influence of Croce on his thought. But for our purposes it is more important to point out that, although this tendency characterizes his thought throughout its development, there is evidence that Collingwood occasionally doubted the validity of the notion that history and philosophy are one and the same thing. In moments of self-criticism, he came back to his earlier notion that the relation between the two realms was one of mere proximity. Regarded from the perspective of its approach to the relation between history and philosophy, Collingwood's thought shows a marked vacillation between several different notions thereof. To criticize Collingwood's ultimate conception of this relation, it would suffice

---

[10] *Ibid.*
[11] Cf. Collingwood's Chapter VI: "Philosophy as Categorical Thinking".
[12] *Religion and Philosophy*, p. 51.

to trace the vacillation characterizing his speculation on this subject and to expose the self-criticism which it reflects.

Before turning to examine Collingwood's own reasons for questioning the validity of his assumption that history and philosophy are identical, let us first consider an objection which he overlooked. Underlying Collingwood's identification of history with philosophy is the assumption that the province of history and philosophy alike is "the totality of existence," or "all that has happened and is happening." The question is whether this assumption is compatible with the nature of either history or philosophy. To answer this question it should be observed that Collingwood could not make this assumption without totally disregarding the material aspect of history, an aspect which he would later take into account. Regarded in terms of its material or thematic content, the province of history is *human* reality. Now, to limit the province of history by linking it with a specific theme, is to preclude the possibility of identifying history and philosophy. For, by contrast with history, philosophy is defined not in terms of a specific theme but in terms of a total scope. That philosophy is defined by reference to totality, Collingwood rightly emphasizes again and again; his *Essay on Philosophical Method* is an attempt to formulate a logic of such an all-embracing totality. Collingwood's mistake lies in his attempt to define history also by reference to totality, i.e. by reference to all that has happened and is happening. The function of history is to investigate *res gestae*. Hence it is concerned only with what *has* happened, and not with what *is* happening. In so far as it deals with the field of *res gestae*, history is concerned only with those events, facts, etc., which are meaningful for the present to the extent that the present directs its attention to them.

Having seen that the assumption underlying Collingwood's identification of history and philosophy is incompatible with the nature of history, let us see whether it is compatible with the nature of philosophy. The question is whether, by virtue of its all-encompassing scope, philosophy is concerned with all that has happened and is happening. Does it follow from the total scope of philosophy that the method of philosophy is one of enumeration? To suggest that the method of philosophy consists in listing and adding up an infinity of particular facts, is to suggest that the function of philosophy is to compile an encyclopaedia of facts. While the latter suggestion is alien to Collingwood's conception of philosophy, he could not refute it without abandoning his assumption that philosophy is concerned with all that has happened and is happening.

So much for the argument against the identification of history with philosophy which Collingwood overlooked. His own arguments can be brought to light by an analysis of those writings in which he emphasizes the difference between the two realms. In *Speculum Mentis*, Collingwood explicitly denies the possibility of identifying history with philosophy and criticizes the view that holds history to be more than a "philosophical error." Like the other forms of mind, history must accept the verdict of incompleteness and must not purport to represent totality. Explaining the gulf between history and philosophy in terms of reflection, Collingwood claims that the philosopher knows "what the historian does not know, that his own knowledge of facts is organic to the facts themselves, that his mind is these facts knowing themselves and that these facts are his mind knowing itself."[13] Collingwood's criticism of history is accordingly based upon the assumption that historical activity is void of self-consciousness. Facts are indeed dealt with; but the mind dealing with them remains external to them.

Philosophy, by contrast, is reflective, conceiving of itself as a part of the "World-Spirit." Unlike history, philosophical activity is not external and alien to the world with which it is concerned, but is rather an internal part thereof. This distinction between philosophy and history, as we shall yet have occasion to see, is eventually abandoned by Collingwood. In his late system, he undertakes to demonstrate that history is likewise reflective, thus undermining his own argument against the identification of history with philosophy. Whereas in *Speculum Mentis* Collingwood passes a verdict of incompleteness upon history on the grounds that it is void of reflection, in his later writings he endows history with reflection, so as to facilitate its identification with philosophy.

Collingwood's vacillation regarding the relation between history and philosophy may, then, be summarized as follows: In order to establish the identity of history and philosophy, Collingwood had recourse to the *tertium comparationis* of totality. Realizing that history cannot be correlated with totality because it excludes the historian's mind from its province, Collingwood concluded that history cannot be identified with philosophy. Not satisfied with this conclusion, Collingwood had to undermine the grounds upon which it was based by proving that history is not unreflective.

Before he arrived at the last stage and regained the lost identity, Collingwood passed through a stage in which he conceived the relation

[13] *Speculum Mentis*, p. 295.

between history and philosophy as one of proximity. To support this conception, he argued that both realms had a common interest. It was in this phase of his development that he wrote: "Philosophy, like history, is essentially the assertion of concrete reality, the denial of all abstraction, all generality, everything in the nature of a law or formula."[14] "For this and similar reasons the identification of philosophy with history is far less violent and misleading than its identification with science, religion or art."[15] And: "The absolute mind is an historical whole of which mine is the part."[16] What these statements imply is that the affinity between philosophy and history is based upon the concern with concrete facts which both intellectual activities share. Like history, philosophy abhors abstraction.

It should be remarked that the foundation upon which this notion of the relation between history and philosophy is based, lies in an aspect of history which Collingwood eventually rejected. For his later conception of history involves a criticism of the view expounded in *Speculum Mentis*, i.e. of the view which conceives history as a concern with facts.

4.

A further stage in the development of Collingwood's approach to the relation between history and philosophy is reflected in his paper "The Nature and Aims of a Philosophy of History." Collingwood draws there a clear-cut distinction between history and philosophy, arguing that while history is finite thinking, philosophy is infinite thinking. He does not even claim, as he claimed in *Speculum Mentis*, that history pretends to be total. Now, he presents history as finite thinking for the same reason that in the earlier work he had presented it as incapable of attaining the totality which it arrogated to itself. His thesis now is that

to philosophize about historical thinking is to transcend the monadism of historical thought, to desert monadism for monadology, to see not merely a perspective but the space of perspectives. History is finite thinking because in its concentration upon its object it suppresses the question of its relation to that object; philosophy is infinite thinking because in philosophy the question what its object is coincides with the question of the relation between its object and itself. Philosophy cancels the finitude of history simply by recognizing it.[17]

[14] *Ibid.*, p. 246.
[15] *Ibid.*
[16] *Ibid.*, p. 299.
[17] "The Nature and Aims of a Philosophy of History", pp. 173–174. Compare *Outlines of a Philosophy of Art*, London, 1925, p. 93.

Collingwood employs here the pair of opposite terms, "finitude" and "infinity," in the Hegelian sense, for he uses the term "finitude" to denote the very distance between the object-pole and the subject-pole of history, and the term "infinity" to denote the all-embracing sphere wherein the two poles are interrelated in such a way as to eliminate their isolation, independence and self-sufficiency. Philosophy, then, is at once thinking of the object and the object thought of. It is neither thinking void of an object, which would be empty thought, nor an object asserted without thinking, which would lead to dogmatic thought. Being essentially reflective, philosophy is infinite. Being essentially naïve, i.e. object-centred, history is finite.

Distinguishing between philosophy and history, Collingwood does not mean to imply that the two realms are unrelated. He maintains that philosophy fulfills a twofold function in relation to history. The first function, which might be called epistemological, is described as "a critical discussion of this attitude, its presuppositions and its implications."[18] The second function, which might be called systematic, is described as "an attempt to discover its place in human experience as a whole, its relation to other forms of experience, its origin and validity."[19] This description of the twofold function of philosophy is reminiscent of the plan which Collingwood had executed in *Speculum Mentis*, where – as we have seen – philosophy fulfills its epistemological and systematic functions in relation to all the diverse forms of experience. By emphasizing these two functions of philosophy in the present context, Collingwood underlines the respective aspects in which it differs from history. Since history does not even pretend to be a form equal in status with philosophy, the question whether history can be identified with philosophy does not arise at all.

The difference between the phases of Collingwood's thought reflected in *Speculum Mentis* and in "The Nature and Aims of a Philosophy of History" may be summarized as follows: In the latter, Collingwood concentrates on the difference between the positions occupied by philosophy and history respectively in the totality of forms of experience. In the earlier work, he also elevated philosophy to a position distinct from that occupied by the other forms. But there he endeavoured to show how philosophy evolved out of the chain-like series of forms, in conformity with a dialectical principle. In "The Nature and Aims of a Philosophy of History" Collingwood makes no mention of this dia-

---

[18] "The Nature and Aims of the Philosophy of History", p. 162.
[19] *Ibid.*

lectical emergence of philosophy from the less complete forms (among which history is included). Here he stresses only the difference in status between history and philosophy.

5.

Still another phase in the development of Collingwood's approach to the relation between history and philosophy is reflected in his *Essay on Philosophical Method*.[20] Collingwood does not explicitly base the distinction which he draws between history and philosophy upon the difference between the subject-object relation characteristic of each realm. At first glance, the distinction which he draws in this work seems to be based upon merely secondary characteristics of history and philosophy, namely the relation of historical and philosophical writing respectively to the writer on the one hand, and to the reader on the other. But if we examine Collingwood's argument more closely, the seemingly secondary characteristics he describes turn out to be essential aspects of the forms under consideration. Let us begin with his description of historical writing: "All historical writing is primarily addressed to a reader, and a relatively uninformed reader; it is therefore instructive or didactic in style ... the writer, however conscientiously he cites authorities, never lays bare the processes of thought which have lead him to his conclusions."[21] Are these aspects of historical writing purely a matter of style or of external form? Or do they rather follow from the very nature of history? Though Collingwood himself does not elucidate the systematic foundation in which the didacticism of historical writing is anchored, this foundation can be exposed by relating what we have learned now to what we learned before about the nature of history. The didacticism of history, its orientation to the reader, and its concealment of the historian's thought-processes, are reflections of what might be called the "extrovert" character of history. In other words, the form of historical writing reflects the nature of history as an activity which proceeds from the knower to the object of his knowledge. In history the knower is, as it were, submerged in the object. Hence there is no need to lay bare his thought-processes, these being regarded as unessential, provisional procedures whose proper place is, so to speak, in the historian's "kitchen."

---

[20] Oxford, 1933.
[21] *An Essay on Philosophical Method*, p. 209.

Let us now turn to Collingwood's description of philosophical writing. By contrast with historical writing, every piece of philosophical writing is primarily addressed to the author himself. It is not by chance that philosophy has been described, metaphorically, as the dialogue of the soul. The metaphor is consonant with the essentially reflective nature of philosophy. Or, as Collingwood puts it, "what we demand of the historian is a product of his thought, what we demand of the philosopher is his thought itself."[22] In other words, while history expresses itself in statements and summaries of facts, philosophy finds expression in the very process of inquiry. The historian relates facts in the form of clear points or material assertions because in history Spirit manifests itself in the form of facts. The philosopher relates his thought-processes because in philosophy Spirit manifests itself in the dynamic form of thought or in the inner movement of thought. The factual crystallizations of Spirit find adequate expression in the statements which the historian makes with a view to instructing the relatively uninformed reader. The dialectical movement of mind finds adequate expression in the dialectic of reflection which might be called its "subjective correlative."

Though in the *Essay on Philosophical Method* Collingwood stresses only the subjective difference in attitude and style which distinguishes historical writing from philosophical writing, it is also possible to distinguish between the two modes of writing on the basis of corresponding differences in their respective objects. But the point which should be stressed is that Collingwood's argument in this work illuminates the difference between history and philosophy from still another point of view, thus bringing even more into relief the shortcomings of the former in relation to the all-embracing system of mind and knowledge.

6.

The final phase in Collingwood's vacillating view concerning the relation between history and philosophy is reflected in his attempt to transfer the object of history from the realm of facts to the realm of thought. By asserting that the object of history is thought, Collingwood sought to re-establish the epistemological possibility of identifying history with philosophy. If the object of history is thought, his argument runs, then it is not a sheer fact but a reflective fact. And if the historical object is a reflective fact, then the nature of history ap-

[22] *Ibid.*, p. 211.

proximates the nature of philosophy *qua* reflection. But this line of
reasoning raises as many problems as it solves.

Having transferred the object of history from the realm of mere facts
to the realm of thought, Collingwood came up against a number of
problems, all of which are connected with the danger of historicism.
That the danger of historicism is immanent in Collingwood's system
has been shown by T. M. Knox.[23] It can also be shown that, in a sense,
Collingwood's identification of history with philosophy constitutes an
attempt to overcome the latent historicism of his thought. But first
it is necessary to explain why the transfer of the historical object to
the realm of thought opens the door to historicism. The explanation
might be formulated as follows: The object of history remains a fact
even after it has been transferred to the realm of thought. Being a fact,
it emerges in a specific situation. That the historical object's factuality
and consequent enmeshment in a specific situation is not overcome by
its nature as thought, seems to be suggested by Collingwood's definition
of "historical questions" as questions concerning "what absolute presuppositions have been made on certain occasions." Now, if historical
questions are questions which arise on specific occasions, then it is always possible to consider every thought as merely a particular thought.
Consequently, thought is dissolved into a plurality of entities, which
plurality is connected with shifting historical circumstances. This con-
sequence is implied by Collingwood's statement that "it is only when
a man's historical consciousness has reached a certain point of maturity
that he realizes how very different have been the ways in which different sets of people have thought."[24]

Further evidence of Collingwood's tendency to correlate thought
with the particular situation in which it emerges, is afforded by his
assertion that "A study of mind on the historical method involves two
renunciations. First it renounces with Locke all 'science of substance.'
It does not ask what mind is; it asks only what mind does."[25] Underlying this assertion is a functional approach to mind which leads to
the notion that there is nothing permanent in thought. This functional
approach atomizes the realm of thought, leaving nothing which is valid
for all sets of people. Thus by transferring the historical object from
the realm of facts to the realm of thought, Collingwood does not cancel

---

[23] Editor's Preface to *The Idea of History*, pp. vii ff.; compare Leo Strauss "On Collingwood's Philosophy of History", *The Review of Metaphysics*, Vol. V/4, 1952, pp. 559–586.
[24] *An Essay on Metaphysics*, Oxford, 1940, p. 56.
[25] *The New Leviathan*, p. 61.

its factuality and particularity, and consequently does not alter the distinguishing marks which he had hitherto ascribed it.

This is not the most serious difficulty inherent in Collingwood's approach to the relation between history and philosophy. A far graver problem is this: thought which is enmeshed in specific and particular situations cannot be evaluated by objective criteria. Void of structure or – to use Collingwood's term – substance, thought becomes essentially Heraclitean. Paradoxically enough, Collingwood ascribes a Heraclitean essence to the very realm which Plato regarded as capable of overcoming Heraclitus.

Collingwood's recourse to the *tertium comparationis*, might be likened to the physician's recourse to the "homeopathic" cure. Though his definition of history as the history of thought is attended by an immanent threat of historicism, Collingwood believes that in the nature of thought there is an element capable of overcoming, or at least mitigating, that threat. While history is indeed concerned with acts of mind which occurred on certain occasions, at the same time it is *mind* that is the agent of those acts. And mind differs from mere experiencing because "experiencing never experiences itself as experiencing."[26] Unlike experiencing, thought is reflective: it is "not mere immediate experience but always reflection or self-knowledge, as the knowledge of oneself as living in these activities."[27] Hence, despite its connection with and enmeshment in a particular situation thought overcomes its particularity by knowing itself as confined to the particular situation in which it is enmeshed. To put this argument of Collingwood's in Hegelian terms one can say that, while by its enmeshment in a particular situation thought is rendered finite, at the same time – by its self-knowledge as enmeshed in that particular situation and, consequently, as finite – thought renders itself infinite.

Because it allows not only for the connection of thought with particular occasions, but also for the transcendence of those particular occasions by thought, this Hegelian argument serves, in a sense, as a means of overcoming historicism. This argument, however, does not imply the existence of a permanent structure or substance of mind. All it implies is a permanent function of thought. "Only what mind does" manages to transcend the confinement of thought to particular occasions. The question is whether the problem of historicism is indeed solved, or whether it is only shifted to another sphere, by Collingwood's

26 *The Idea of History*, p. 294.
27 *Ibid.*, p. 297.

assumption that the particularity of thought is transcended by, and only by, the perpetual activity of thought. Is historicism overcome if the content of thought remains irremediably enmeshed in particular situations? Strangely enough, Collingwood seems to think that the problem of historicism can be solved by assuming that nothing is permanent in mind but the process of mind itself.

Another tenet of Collingwood's system which may be regarded as a means of evading the historicist pitfall is the notion that in the realm of history, thought is reflective in two respects. In the first place, it is reflective because the historical agent who entertains a particular thought, transcends its particularity by an act of reflection. In the second place, it is reflective because the historian directs his attention to, and re-enacts, the thoughts entertained by historical agents on particular occasions in the past. This is what Collingwood has in mind when he writes that "history does not mean knowing what events flowed from what" but "getting inside other peoples' heads, looking at their situation through their eyes, and thinking for yourself whether the way in which they tackled it was the right way."[28] In other words, two acts of transcendence are required in order to reflect upon the thought entertained by an historical agent. By the first act, the historian transcends the particular situation in which the thought occurred to get inside the head of the historical agents. By the second act, he transcends the thought of those agents by thinking for himself whether the means they employed to attain their ends were appropriate.

It might be worth mentioning in passing that Collingwood criticizes Bergson because his philosophy does not allow for reflection and because without reflection "there can be no history; for history is not immediate self-enjoyment, it is reflection, meditation, thought. It is an intellectual labour whose purpose is to think the life of the mind instead of merely enjoying. But according to Bergson's philosophy this is impossible; what is inward can only be enjoyed, not thought."[29] In our context, however, it is more important to note that Collingwood's purpose in rendering history reflective, is to overcome historicism. By re-enacting, and thus transcending, the thought of an historical agent in the past, the historian endows it with a new mode of universality. The factual thought which constitutes the historian's object is universal not in the sense of being *valid* beyond the circumstances under which it occurred; but in the sense of being meaningful beyond those

---

[28] *An Autobiography*, p. 43.
[29] *The Idea of History*, pp. 188–189.

circumstances. The universality of its meaning is witnessed by the very fact that the historian can direct his attention towards it and re-enact it in himself. The question, however, is whether by endowing the historical object *qua* thought with universal meaningfulness, Collingwood evaded the historicist pitfall.

To overcome historicism, it is necessary to guarantee not only the universal meaningfulness, but also the universal validity of thought. And to guarantee validity, it does not suffice to guarantee meaningfulness. In so far as positivism tends to identify meaning with validity and validity with verifiability, Collingwood's identification of history with philosophy may be regarded as a means of evading the positivistic pitfall. This identification safeguards the meaning, but not the validity, of the historical object *qua* thought. Validity can be established only by principles that are binding; it cannot be established by thoughts that are enmeshed in particular historical situations. The relation between historicism and positivism, a relation anchored in a common philosophical heritage and in common systematic presuppositions, is a well-known fact. But from this relation it does not follow that an evasion of the positivistic pitfall is *ipso facto* an evasion of the historicist pitfall. Though he may have overcome positivism, Collingwood clearly never overcame historicism; for in his mature system, as expounded in the *Essay on Metaphysics*, he explicitly adheres to the historicist assumption that "the question of what presuppositions underlie the 'physics' or natural science of a certain people at a certain time, is as purely historical a question as what kind of clothes they wear."[30]

7.

Collingwood's failure to overcome the danger of historicism might be explained as follows: by identifying history with philosophy he not only elevated history to a philosophical plane but also – and by the same stroke – relegated philosophy to an historical plane. It is true that Collingwood does not define philosophy in terms of a specific theme or subject-matter. But neither does he define it in terms of its structure, as he had defined it in his *Essay on Philosophical Method*. In his late system, philosophy is defined as a mode of activity, i.e. as reflective thought. This definition may perhaps be regarded as an

---

[30] *An Autobiography*, p. 48. See the present author's "Metaphysics and Historicism", in the volume *Critical Essays on the Philosophy of R. G. Collingwood* mentioned before.

expression of Collingwood's functional approach to philosophy, which approach is based upon an historical, or historicist, method. But what is more significant is that by defining philosophy as reflective thought, Collingwood relegated it to the plane of history, thus diverting the danger of historicism from the historical to the philosophical realm.

Philosophy is rendered vulnerable to historicism by the very attempt to render history invulnerable to it. Unlike history, philosophy is not exposed to the danger of historicism by its very nature. For philosophy is not merely reflective thought, but reflective thought about principles. Being active, and accordingly binding, those principles are valid. And the validity of the principles to which it is oriented guarantees the validity of philosophy and immunizes it against historicism. Judging from his *Essay on Metaphysics*, Collingwood was aware of the relation between philosophy and principles, though in that work he was concerned with the existence of the philosophical domain rather than with its validity. Be this as it may, the point is that, by identifying philosophy with history, Collingwood exposed it to the danger of an historicist invasion. Thus he sacrificed the safety of philosophy in an effort to safeguard history from a danger to which it is exposed by its very nature.[31]

It is worth mentioning that Collingwood's aim in identifying history with philosophy was not only to overcome historicism but also to attack psychologism. If the real object of history is mind, then it is not psychology, but history which offers an adequate account of the nature of mind. Psychologism tends to transform mind into a series of acts and to ignore the thought or content inherent in mind. In other words, the psychologistic approach to mind regards it as an activity of immediate experiencing only. This approach accordingly robs mind of its *differentia specifica*, reflection. And, as Collingwood rightly observes, "the mind, regarded in this way, ceases to be a mind at all."[32] Given the relation between psychologism and historicism (which relation, by the way, prompted Husserl to attack both in his *Philosophie als strenge Wissenschaft*) one may regard Collingwood's direct criticism of the former as an indirect criticism of the latter.

Still another tenet of Collingwood's system which is explicitly designed to overcome the danger of historicism, is his notion that the authentic historical attitude is an attitude of practical engagement.

---

[31] See the present author's *Spirit and Man, An Essay on Being and Value*, The Hague, 1963.
[32] *An Autobiography*, p. 65.

Unlike the historicist attitude, which is contemplative, uncommitted, and strictly intellectual in its understanding of life, the historical attitude – as defined by Collingwood – involves active participation in the solutions of life's problems.

The scissors-and-paste men think differently: they think that first of all people get into the habit of reading books and then the books put questions into their heads. But I am not talking about scissors-and-paste history. In the kind of history I am thinking of, the kind I have been practising all my life, historical problems arise out of practical problems. We study history in order to see more clearly into the situation in which we are called upon to act.[33]

...In re-thinking what somebody else thought, he thinks it himself. In knowing that somebody else thought it, he knows that he himself is able to think it. And finding out what he is able to do is finding out what kind of man he is ... Thus his own self-knowledge is at the same time his knowledge of the world of human affairs.[34]

The historical attitude, in other words, realizes the Socratic imperative, "know thyself." Unlike Socrates, however, Collingwood does not believe that in itself self-knowledge is a mode of practice; knowledge is a mode of practice; knowledge is prerequisite to solving practical problems. To solve those problems – so his argument runs – we must commit ourselves by making decisions. Our decisions carry us beyond the sphere of contemplative understanding, to involve us in the practical activity of shaping the actual course of our lives. To put this anti-historicist argument of Collingwood's in another way, the end of historical reflection is action; and action is incompatible with historicism by its very nature. Though our actions are prompted by particular circumstances, they transcend those circumstances through their orientation to the creation of situations which do not as yet exist.

In contrast to the historicist attitude, which is oriented to the past, practical action is oriented to the future. By opening the horizon of the future, historical understanding overcomes the danger of historicism in the sense of an exclusive orientation to the past. The parallelism between this argument of Collingwood and that employed by Marx in his attack against historicism is worthy of notice, though Collingwood himself was unaware of it. Be this as it may, the point to be borne in mind is that, in the last analysis, practice is Collingwood's only refuge from the danger of historicism immanent in his system. His theory, as we have seen, succumbs to this danger despite his efforts to overcome it.

To conclude, it might be appropriate to review the main phases of

[33] *Ibid.*, p. 78. Compare Collingwood's assertion that "all thought exists for the sake of action", in *Speculum Mentis*, p. 15.

[34] *An Autobiography*, pp. 78–79. Compare Collingwood's assertion that "the value of history is that it teaches us what man has done and what man is", in *The Idea of History*, p. 10.

Collingwood's vacillating approach to the relation between philosophy and history. Whereas in the earlier phase Collingwood underlined the differences between the two realms, in the later phase he tried to establish their identity. To identify history with philosophy, he had to abandon the conception of history upon which he had based his distinction between them. And by altering his conception of the nature of history, he also altered his conception of the status which it occupies in the system of mind. In contrast to his conception of history, Collingwood's conception of philosophy underwent no changes as a result of his vacillating approach. Throughout all the phases of his development he correlated philosophy with totality; totality of structure (identity of subject and object), and totality of scope (synoptic encompassment of all the diverse forms of mind). But in the later phase, when it is identified with history, philosophy is exposed to a danger to which it had hitherto been immune, the danger of historicism. The problem presented by the historicist threat to philosophy – a problem Collingwood did not cope with – is whether an historicist conception of totality is not a contradiction in terms.

C. ISSUES

I. *Ways of Cognition*

a) Concurrently with the changes which took place in Collingwood's understanding of the nature of history and its systematic status, as analysed before, there occurred a change in his account of the ways of historical cognition. Here the system exhibits the full compass of modes of knowledge starting with perception and winding up with "re-enact-ment." We shall consider now the various forms of cognition suggested, and try to analyse the reasons which periodically drove Collingwood to seek another, more adequate, form of historical cognition. A criticism of his various attempts will accompany our analysis.

"In perception we are immediately aware of our object, which is a historical fact: perception and history are thus identical."[1] This state-ment is not altogether exact, since Collingwood does not identify the historical *object* with perception. He identifies historical *knowledge*, or more exactly, the *medium* of historical knowledge with perception. Per-ception is that form of awareness which in its very essence is object-centred. To be sure, even in this stage of his system Collingwood does not consider perception to be an immediate awareness only. In Hegelian vein he says: "Perception is explicitly immediate, but it always con-tains within itself a mediation (thought, 'interpretation of sense data', inference from the immediately given, or whatever one likes to call it) and is never abstract immediacy."[2] Again, in Kantian terms, Colling-wood talks about the "judgement" which is implicit in a perception. Thus he precludes the possibility of identifying perception with mere experience *qua* an affection of the passive knower by the object.

Yet even when Collingwood considers perception to be the element of historical consciousness and stresses in the nature of perception the

---

[1] *Speculum Mentis*, p. 204.
[2] *Ibid.*, p. 205.

awareness of the given object, he goes beyond perception, though maintaining the term "perception." Unless we quarrel about terminology it would be hard to consider as perception the kind of reconstruction which Collingwood puts on it. "To perceive is to see what we do not see, to grasp the object as a whole in a synthesis of front and back, top and bottom, past, present, and future; all this is implied in my perception of the ink-pot I see before me. Thus in perception we have that very identical process of reconstruction from data which is the essence of history."[3] In perception we go beyond the actual immediate experience; we also know what is not actually given. Thus perception is already an act or an active enlargement of the given datum. It is an act of synthesis. If perception is a synthetic or constructive act, it at once eliminates the object-centred quality of historical knowledge. We may even say that historical knowledge is objectively outside the object-centred stage of the mind in its very various manifestations, without however being aware that it implicitly transcends the object. There is implicit in historical knowledge a tipping of the scale *a parte subjecti*, but the subject himself is not yet aware of this preponderance. From this point of view, perception is perception only, and lacks apperception, to use the well-known distinction of Leibniz.

It is indeed this quality of perception that later led Collingwood to doubt the capacity of perception to serve as the mode of knowledge characteristic of history. It is true that at least once in his later writings he referred again to the relation between history and perception, maintaining that historical thought is in one way "like perception."[4] The *tertium comparationis* between historical knowledge and perception according to this view is that both are concerned with individual facts. Yet Collingwood became aware of the fundamental difference between perception and the nature of historical knowledge. Perception, in spite of the synthesis and the reconstruction involved in it, is confined to what is given in the present. Perception is the awareness of the present. In contra-distinction to it, "historical thought is of something which can never be this, because it is never here and now. Its object are events which have finished happening, and conditions no longer in existence. Only when they are no longer perceptible do they become objects of historical thought."[5] Historical knowledge is thus different from knowledge through perceptive acquaintance, since its object is never a given

---

[3] *Ibid.*, p. 212.
[4] *The Idea of History*, p. 283.
[5] *Ibid.*

fact. Thus the precondition of the identification of historical knowledge with perception is absent. This limitation of perception was not
considered in *Speculum Mentis*, since there Collingwood did not deal
with the problem of the relation between past and present in the framework of his system. One may even say that in his early system Collingwood's attitude to history was a naïve one. He simply pointed to the
awareness of the object in historical knowledge, although he already
stressed the activity of the subject involved. But the existence of the
object and the reference to the existing object was a kind of axiomatic
assumption in his examination of the nature of historical knowledge. It
was here that the important change in Collingwood's attitude occurred,
a change which led him to a new approach to the entire problem: once
the historical object is not understood as given, once it is reconstructed
not in *some* of its facets, but in its *entire* status, it becomes impossible
to consider perception as the adequate medium of historical cognition.

This can be expressed from another angle as well: according to the
new view of the nature of history, history is not concerned with events
but with thought. Events, i.e. external occurrences, are the concern of
geology. History has an entirely different object of investigation. Historical events are inaccessible to any kind of observation, since they
are placed on an ontologically different level; "the inner side of the
event"[6] does not lend itself to being perceived. It requires a new medium
of cognition. To summarize this view we may say that as long as Collingwood considered the distinctive feature of history to be precisely its
reference to objects, he held historical knowledge to be based on perception. But this view was given up because of a twofold consideration:
In terms of the time-dimension, the historical object is not simply given
in the present and hence in order to be known it must be reconstructed.
This kind of reconstruction is different from that already involved in
perception; this is not a reconstruction in order to complete the picture
or the shape of the object, its top and bottom, etc.; this is a reconstruction which goes beyond the present and attempts to conceive something
which is not present. On the other hand, the material nature of the
object *qua* thought requires a cognitive activity which will be adequate
to it. Perception may not be this adequate activity.

b) There is in Collingwood's words an incidental reference to the status
of memory in historical knowledge. It has already been pointed out
that in the later stage of Collingwood's system the time-gap between the

6 *Ibid.*, p. 222.

knower and the objects of his knowledge precludes the connection of history with perception as its cognitive medium. It is precisely this time-gap which is bridged in memory, and this is probably the reason which led Collingwood to connect history with memory, in spite of the serious doubts that have been entertained about this connection, for instance by Oakeshott.[7] "The gap of time between my present thought and its past object is bridged not by the survival or revival of the object, but only by the power of thought to overlap such a gap; and the thought which does this is memory."[8] And yet again: "Historical knowledge is that special case of memory where the object of present thought, the gap between present and past being bridged not by the power of present thought to think of the past, but also by the power of past thought to reawaken itself in the present."[9] There is a slight difference between the two statements concerning the status and the importance of memory in history: in the first, Collingwood stresses that it is the present thought which goes towards the past, and in the second he stresses the reciprocity in the relationship between the past thought and the present, a reciprocity existing in memory. The emphasis on this reciprocity expresses Collingwood's view more truly than the conception of a one-sided activity on the part of the present thought. In any case, the activity of the knower is implied more in memory than in perception, in spite of Collingwood's own attempt to interpret perception as an activity. But it seems that memory cannot be considered as a form of historical cognition, that is to say, as a medium through or by which the past object is conceived. Memory can at most be considered as the *background* for historical cognition, that is to say, as the factor providing for the continuity within the passing process, which is the precondition for the establishment of the relation between the past and the present. It is clear that perception cannot do this; but neither can memory, for memory may be considered as the medium for a form of cognition, but not as a cognition in itself.[10] Hence, Collingwood continues to search for a more adequate form of historical cognition and suggests at least two modes: imagination and re-enactment.

c) The first step which Collingwood makes to break through the limits of perception as the medium of historical knowledge is to relate his-

[7] Michael Oakeshott, *Experience and its Modes*, Cambridge, 1933, p. 86.
[8] *The Idea of History*, p. 203.
[9] *Ibid.*, p. 294.
[10] Compare "Memory is an implication, not the definition, of the historical consciousness", *Speculum Mentis*, p. 212.

torical knowledge to imagination. What brings Collingwood to establish this relation in spite of the fact that he retains the idea that imagination is the form of art, whereas history is considered to be a higher form of mind than art? One might suggest the following reasons for consideration:

(1) The productive or active aspect, which has already been stressed as present in perception, is the main feature of imagination: it is a cognition manifesting the activity of the knowing subject. In imagination the relation of subject and object is one in which the subject assumes predominance. The object is not given; it is constructed. Once Collingwood became aware of the difficulty implied in the consideration of historical knowledge as connected with perception, which is essentially a perception of something present, he took refuge in imagination.

(2) Clearly there is present in imagination a feature which seems rather strange in terms of the early system, where historical knowledge amounted to the assertion of facts and where the dogmatism rooted in history was realism. Once history becomes connected with imagination, it clearly ceases to be realistic. To imagine an object is to detach oneself from its reality and not to attach to it an imaginary feature of unreality. The product of imagination is not the opposite, but the imaginary equivalent, of the real.[11] The reality of the historical picture retained its hold on Collingwood's mind even after he connected history with imagination, and this contributes to a certain perplexity in his mature system.

(3) In imagination we go beyond mere experience, taken in the sense of impression. Actually the world of the empiricist is not the world of atomized impressions, and once we transcend sensation we reach imagination. Imagination is like a third factor, in Kantian terms, mediating between mere sensation and pure thought. There is in imagination a facet which brings it close both to sensation, since it refers to particular phenomena, and to thought: in imagination we overcome the confinement to what is actually, here and now, present. In imagination the object is known although it is not immediately before the mind. Thus the time horizon of imagination is broader than that of perception. Therefore imagination can provide that bridge between the present and the past which was wanting in perception. The indifference towards reality, the non-commitment of imagination as to the reality or unreality of its object, is what renders it possible to envisage imagination as the medium of historical knowledge.

[11] Cf. *The Principles of Art*, Oxford, 1937, p. 136.

(4) The systematic exposition of imagination points to one of its features which must in turn annihilate its status in historical knowledge. "The conception of past, future, the possible, the hypothetical, are as meaningless for imagination as they are for feeling itself. They are conceptions which appear only with a further development of thought."[12] If the gap between the dimension of time and the awareness of them cannot be bridged by imagination, it will be hard to assume the value of imagination for history. Collingwood did not return, in the later stage of his development, to this aspect of imagination, presumably on the grounds that once we talk about *historical* imagination, we assume that its special task is to "imagine the past."[13]

(5) The enlargement of the scope of what is actually sensed has been considered already as a feature of perception:"... perceptual imagination presents objects of possible perception which are not actually perceived: the underside of this table."[14] Even the example used is almost the same as that which has been mentioned in relation to perception (see above). The difference between perception and imagination will therefore be this: imagination can be related to the past, while perception can be related to the present only. Or in other words: for imagination, the past is like "the underside of the table," conceived as real although not actually given here and now.

(6) Historical knowledge, as knowledge of thoughts expressed in acts, is now conceived as a construction and not as a mere assertion of facts as in the early view. The constructive feature of historical knowledge is emphasized in the term *imagination*.

(7) But once Collingwood takes advantage of imagination he comes close to art and must face the problem of the relation between history and art. "Freed from its dependence on fixed points supplied from without, the historian's picture of the past is thus in every detail an imaginary picture ... whatever goes into it, goes into it not because his imagination passively accepts it, but because it actively demands it."[15] Active construction, though, poses the question of the difference between the picture painted by the historian and that by the novelist.

(8) "As works of imagination, the historian's work and the novelist's do not differ."[16] Yet Collingwood cannot disregard the important differ-

---

[12] *Outlines of a Philosophy of Art*, p. 13. Imagination is like the phenomenological *epoche* placing reality "outside the brackets".
[13] *The Principles of Art*, p. 224.
[14] *The Idea of History*, p. 242.
[15] *Ibid.*
[16] *The Idea of History*, p. 245.

ences between the two kinds of work, since a historical work is a work of *knowledge* and not a *mere construction*. Therefore he is compelled to restrict his own statement: "Where they do differ is that the historian's picture is meant to be true. The novelist has a single task only: to construct a coherent picture, one that makes sense. The historian has a double task: he has both to do this and to construct a picture of things as they really were and of events as they really happened."[17] We can observe here an oscillation between the constructive nature of the historical picture and its pretension to be true, or in other words its necessary obedience to the criteria of *truth*. It may be that it is a paradoxical feature in historical knowledge: to be constructive and yet to render an account of what really happened. But one cannot resolve this paradox by saying, on the one hand, that there is no difference between the work of the historian and the work of the novelist, and yet imposing, on the other hand, on the work of the historian rules which do not make sense in the "universe of discourse" of the novelist. In terms of Collingwood's own usage we may say that he connects historical knowledge with imagination, and yet does not give up the categorical or assertive nature of historical statements, as statements about facts. The shift of historical knowledge to the field of imagination is an attempt to overcome the time limits of perception. But once the shift occurs and imagination becomes the means of historical knowledge, the problem of historical knowledge as *knowledge* becomes crucial. Once again we watch here the inner complexity of the philosophy of history as Collingwood understood its nature. The view of *Speculum Mentis* took for granted the existence of the object in history. The shortcomings of history were then assumed to lie in the secondary position of the subject and its being is absorbed in the object. The view expounded in *The Idea of History* safeguards the subject; but the question now is how to provide for the object; otherwise, how can the historical subject overstep his subjectivity? The problem of the position of imagination in historical knowledge makes this perplexity apparent.

To point out the difference between the picture of the novelist and that of the historian, three methodological rules are laid down. These rules hold good in history, but cannot be applied to art:

(a) The picture must be localized in space and in time.

(b) Purely imaginary worlds cannot clash and need not agree: each is a world in itself. But there is only one historical world, and everything in it must stand in some relation to everything else.

[17] *Ibid.*, p. 246.

(c) The historian's picture stands in a peculiar relation to evidence."[18] These three methodological rules are independent of one another, but all of them point to the main feature present in historical knowledge and absent in an historical novel: the going beyond the boundaries of the picture itself. The mere picture itself is supplemented in a twofold way, in the *realistic* aspect of historical knowledge and in the element of *coherence* implied in it. The first and the third methodological rules are realistic in their direction; they point to components which refer the historical picture to facts outside it: the time and space factor and the evidence which establishes the historical picture and provides for its consistence with the happenings themselves. The second methodological rule points to the inner coherence of the historical world. Since this is a *real* world and not a world of fiction, there is bound to be one world only, and there is bound to be, correspondingly, one coherent and all embracing-historical picture of it. The historical novel is fragmentary; it creates its own co-ordinates and does not pretend to be a part of a whole. Actually there are two criteria which provide for the difference between the historical picture and the picture of a novelist, and they can be expressed in terms of the traditional theories of truth: the historical picture must be true in terms of the theory of *correspondence* and the theory of *coherence* as well: it must correspond to evidence and must indicate acts in time and space. But it must be coherent not only within itself but with the entire historical universe. Hence the difference between history and art is that between a fragmentary coherence (which in a sense is a contradiction in terms) and all-embracing coherence. All history must be universal history, as Collingwood put it in one of his early statements.[19] Universality is the concrete materialization of the all-embracing coherence.

We may sum up this discussion of the relation of historical knowledge to imagination as follows: imagination was supposed to overcome the shortcomings of perception and yet to retain its advantage in terms of the truth-value of the statements based on it. Collingwood strove to combine the advantages of both cognitive media: truth taken from perception, and independence taken from imagination. It sounds like an attempt to combine freedom and order in the realm of politics. Yet the problematic nature of this combination is clear in Collingwood's own statements, which are critical in their very essence.

---

[18] *Ibid.*

[19] "History is essentially universal history, a whole in which the knowledge of every fact is included" (*Speculum Mentis*, p. 231).

The introduction of re-enactment as historical cognition, or as *the* form of historical cognition, does not solve the problem inherent in the inner polarity of imagination, but shifts it to a higher level.

d) The assumption that imagination is the means of historical knowledge already presupposes the change in the understanding of history as an object-centred knowledge. The assumption that re-enactment is the means of historical knowledge re-emphasizes the same trend; it even makes it more explicit. The nature of history is defined from the point of view of the knower: "If we raise the question, Of what can there be historical knowledge? the answer is, Of that which can be re-enacted in the historian's mind."[20] Actually, re-enactment is only the act of reflecting the thought which is the object of history, an act accomplished within the thought of the historian.

There is a clear difference between the nature of perception and imagination as means of historical knowledge on the one hand, and, on the other hand, the nature of re-enactment. Perception and imagination are acts of mind with an established status in the scale of acts of mind, while re-enactment is invented *ad hoc* for the sake of historical knowledge as such. When Collingwood connects historical knowledge either with perception or with imagination, he identifies the unknown factor of historical knowledge with one of the known and established factors, either perception or imagination. Re-enactment, however, is but another expression of the nature of historical knowledge as re-thinking of thoughts. Yet this might be a secondary factor only. However, there is a more serious difference to be observed: whereas perception and imagination point to *media* of historical knowledge, re-enactment points rather to the *task* of historical knowledge. This might be the hidden reason why Collingwood considered both imagination and re-enactment to be inherent in historical knowledge, as if he wished to assume that imagination as he understood it was to serve as an organ of re-enactment, which in turn is the essence of historical knowledge. Thus we may distinguish between imagination as the way of cognition, and re-enactment which uses imagination but is more than just a way of cognition. This point, however, remains unclear in Collingwood.

What is the logic of Collingwood's argument which leads to the view that re-enactment is the nature of historical cognition? We may distinguish between two lines of argument, one running from the nature of the historical object, the other from the fact that the only certain

[20] *The Idea of History*, p. 302.

starting-point in historical knowledge is the mind of the historian. The first line is clear: the historian's object is thought. The adequate cognition of thought is re-thought, or re-thinking, as Collingwood prefers to call it, and re-thinking is re-enactment of the former thought of the historical agent in the present thought of the historian. But there is the second line of argument running the other way round. The historical object is that which can be re-enacted in the mind of the historian. Re-enactment is an act of thought: it is thought knowing itself as thought. The object must conform to the nature of its cognition; and therefore it must be thought itself.

Re-enactment as historical cognition led Collingwood to the identification of philosophy and history as analysed before. Collingwood, in a Hegelian way, connected philosophical thought with self-consciousness. Once consciousness becomes self-consciousness, it establishes the closed totality which is expressed in philosophy. Or to put it differently, the characteristic feature of philosophy is the awareness of the identity between subject and object. The locus of this identity is self-consciousness, where the subject knows himself. There is no way of establishing the identity of subject and object other than by their ontological identity, within the realm of the subject who knows himself as his own object. Reflection as *knowledge of knowledge* is the manifestation in terms of cognition of the fundamental ontological identity of subject and object. The ontological identity of subject and object does not carry with itself any division in terms of time: subject and object differ dialectically but do not differ chronologically. They are identical in spite of their difference, not as an outcome of a development in time, but as a result of the exposition of the very essence of the related poles.

Now, within the realm of history, the identity of subject and object poses serious difficulties. The object is the historical action, and the subject is the historian. What kind of identity can be established here in spite of the ontological difference between the poles and in spite of the time-gap between them? The concept of re-enactment was introduced in order to solve these problems and to provide the cognitive ground for the establishment of the identity between philosophy and history. How could this be accomplished?

In the first place, the ontological difference between object and subject is not a fundamental one. It does not matter at all that the object is one historical individual and the knower another human being. The difference between the poles is one within the realm of the unity and identity of man, while the "biographical" difference in terms of time is metaphysically an irrelevant factor. Thus when an historian in the twentieth century considers a thought of an historical agent in the fifth century B.C. in Athens, he serves only as the medium of the self-awareness of humanity. This identity in nature, the metaphysical element embracing the difference, solves the second difficulty in terms of the time-gap as well. The time-gap is an accidental factor. Re-enactment as historical reflection, re-enactment in history as the equivalent of the self-reflective nature of self-consciousness, stresses the ontological identity of subject and object in history, an identity similar to that present in dialectical philosophy.

Assuming that re-enactment and reflection are identical in terms of function, are they identical in terms of their respective content? Does it make sense to assume that historical re-enactment is a re-enactment of a purposive thought concerned with the theoretical-synoptic picture of the universe? A thought re-enacted in history must be a thought of a purposive nature, according to Collingwood's own view. Shall we assume that philosophical thought is purposive as well, even in its expression as *synopsis*? Philosophical thought is a *theoretical* reflection, while historical thought in terms of the historical agent is a *purposive* activity. Even when the historian re-enacts in his inquiry a purposive thought of an historical agent, he has to re-enact the purpose of that thought and cannot interpret it as a pure theory (in the ancient sense of *theoria*) in terms of philosophy. This is a limit put on historical knowledge by the nature of the object concerned, and no subjective approach to history can overcome the ontological-material nature of its object. In order to assume the identity between philosophical reflection and historical re-enactment, one has in the first place to understand philosophical activity itself as a purposive or as a pragmatic activity. One wonders if this would be Collingwood's conception, since even pragmatists hesitate to abolish the theoretical nature of the pragmatist philosophy *qua* philosophy.

If the historical object is thought, as is historical re-enactment, then the historical object itself is already a reflection, since reflection is of the nature of thought. Thus in history there is really a double reflection, as it were: one within the realm of the object, and the other within the scope of the historian's mind. If reflection is already present in the scope of the object, what is historical knowledge for – at all? A philosophical system once created by and through the reflection of a philosopher is a part of "the objective mind," whether or not it is re-

reflected by a student of philosophy in a subsequent period of time. But according to Collingwood's own presupposition, an historical action becomes historical only when it is re-enacted by the historian, or only when it leaves some traces which are reconstructed by an historian. Thus an historical object, in spite of the fact that it is thought, needs explicitly a knower *different* from itself; only if the knower is different, can history be a meaningful cognitive activity at all. The identity of subject and object emphasized by Collingwood in order to assure the *rapprochement* between philosophy and history, overshadows the most important feature of historical knowledge, namely that the knower is different from what he knows. In philosophy, man, in spite of being a particular psychosomatic individual living in a particular setting in terms of time and space, faces the universe. In history, an individual belonging to one generation faces an agent belonging to a previous generation, and this time-difference is the *raison-d'être* of history. If re-enactment were less pretentious in its nature than Collingwood assumed it to be, it could serve as one of the indications of the *sympathetic* nature of historical knowledge. But since it has this pretension and presumably aspires to a position similar to that of the reflective self-consciousness in philosophy, it leads to a confusion as to the real nature of history.

Collingwood himself was aware of the problem of the distance between subject and object in history, and he attempted to solve this problem in a very significant way. Let us first quote at some length a passage which throws light on his attitude:

When as an historian, I relive in my own mind a certain experience of Julius Caesar, I am not simply being Julius Caesar; on the contrary, I am myself and know I am myself; the way in which I incorporate Julius Caesar's experience in my own personality is not by confusing myself with him, but by distinguishing myself from him and at the same time making his experience my own. The living past of history lives in the present, but it lives not in the immediate experience of the present, but only in the self-knowledge of the present.[21]

The historian in the present re-enacts the thought of the past agent, but he does not become absorbed into the object of his re-enactment. The object turns out to be absorbed in the present mind of the subject; the subject is therefore independent of the object and, as it were, richer than the past thought. There is thus in history not an identity between subject and object but something additional on the part of the subject. In terms of Collingwood's own systematic development, the wheel has certainly come a full circle: history as considered in *Speculum*

21 *Ibid.*, p. 174.

Mentis, was criticized as absorbing the subject, or rather as not leaving room for the thought of the subject. This has been overcome in the later system, since the realm in which object and subject meet is the subject and his thought, which in terms of the time-dimension is synonymous with the present. But still, there is something in the subject which makes it different from its object, viz. the thought of the subject himself. The knower re-enacts the thought of the historical agent but does not identify himself with that thought. The subject is beyond and outside his object. Thus in the theory of re-enactment two trends, different and colliding in a way, are to be traced: re-enactment presupposes the identity between the knower and his object, yet the knower is beyond his object and thus not identical with it. The dialectic between the identity and the difference present in historical knowledge and within re-enactment is implicit in Collingwood's view, and as it happens in Collingwood's system, one aspect of it criticizes the other. What is remarkable in the theory of re-enactment is that this tension between the trends is not one between two chronological stages in the systematic development of Collingwood's philosophy, but rather within one and the same theory belonging to one and the same phase of his system.

Collingwood's system considered from the aspect of the suggested means for historical cognition, progressed all the way from perception through imagination to re-enactment. It leaves us with the unsolved problem of the nature of a "bounded" imagination and with the problem of the dialectical nature of re-enactment. The system implies the identity between the knower and his object and yet it assumes the preponderance of the knower.

2. *Datum*

a) It has been shown that in Collingwood's system the problem of the direction of historical cognition may be summed up as the problem of the relation between the commitment of historical knowledge to facts on the one hand, and the freedom of that knowledge from restriction on the other. As the natural counterpart of this line of thought, the problem of the historical datum arises.

The interpretation of the nature of historical knowledge as a knowledge concerned with facts was the main characteristic of history in the early stage of Collingwood's system. This interpretation links historical knowledge to, and makes it dependent upon, a factor which is beyond knowledge. One of the main motives that led Collingwood to re-formulate his early view lies in his realization that the question involves the problem of the accessibility of facts. This problem can be considered from two angles:

(1) "The alleged facts upon which it builds its inductions are actually never secure enough to bear the weight that is put upon them."[22] "No fact ever has been wholly ascertained, but a fact may be progressively ascertained."[23] Thus the fixed point of historical knowledge according to the *simpliste* view propounded early ceases to be a fixed point at all and is itself included within the setting of historical knowledge. The *simpliste* view bases historical knowledge on facts outside knowledge itself and is thus realistic in its trend. Once this view has been rejected on the grounds that the "real facts" can never be ascertained, the problem arises as to whether historical knowledge is free in its nature, or whether within its own scope a distinction can be made between cognition and that to which cognition in its manifestation *qua* imagination refers; in other words, where does cognition originate? The introduction of the "fact factor" into the scope of knowledge as such clearly recalls the conception of the Marburg School within the Neo-Kantian movement, where the datum is transferred from the "outside world" and becomes an element of the inner-immanent stimulation within knowledge proper.

(2) The second reason for the inclusion of the factual factor in the scope of knowledge is related to the nature of the historical datum. The datum for historical knowledge is related to the nature of the historical datum. The datum for historical knowledge is never the real fact as it occurred in the past. The datum must be in the present. "What really happened" is simply the thing in itself, the thing defined as out of all relation to the knower of it, not only unknown, not only unknowable but non-existent.[24] Precisely because historical knowledge is knowledge of a datum, the latter must be included within the scope of the knowledge itself. To know the past as it was, means to know that which is beyond the reach of knowledge. Collingwood's formulation of the idealistic argument against the thing in itself, similar to the formulations of the Neo-Kantian Marburg tradition of Hermann Cohen and his followers, is quite radical: it is not only *unknowable* but also *non-existent*. Historical knowledge has a datum on which it must rely, but

[22] "The Nature and Aims of a Philosophy of History", p. 152.
[23] *Ibid.*, p. 160.
[24] "The Limits of Historical Knowledge", *Journal of Philosophical Studies*, Vol. III/10, 1928, p. 219.

precisely because it has a datum it cannot be knowledge of an independent past. Facts are in a past time, while data are in a present time. As a knowledge of data, historical knowledge is a knowledge of the *traces* of facts and not a knowledge of *facts*.

Historical knowledge in this sense relies upon evidence. If there were no evidence, there would be no object to be known. "Historical thinking means nothing else than interpreting all the available evidence with the maximum degree of critical skill."[25] But the fact that historical knowledge rests on evidence, which means, in effect, that it refers to traces of events which must be included in the scope of the historian's universe as objects of interpretation, leads to a skeptical evaluation of historical knowledge: "... this is the root of historical skepticism – we only have a strictly limited quantity of evidence concerning any historical question; it is seldom free from grave defects, it is generally tendentious, fragmentary, silent where it ought to be explicit, and detailed where it had better be silent ..."[26] Historical knowledge relies upon a factor which is never certain. It faces a real dilemma: either it is completely tied to relying on the evidence, the obvious defects of that evidence notwithstanding; or it has to be given up altogether. To overcome this "to be or not to be" of historical knowledge, no other way is open to us than to rely on the evidence of the datum. "In history we must not doubt, we dare not doubt, we must assume that our evidence is adequate, though we know it to be inadequate."[27] We are committed to "an act of irrational acquiescence."[28] Historical knowledge is thus carried out *in spite* of its inherent and justified skepticism. This skepticism might be considered as double: first, historical knowledge does not refer to the object in the past. This might be called a skepticism in terms of the object. Second: historical knowledge, even when related to, and relying on, a datum in the present is never certain, since it expresses itself in a network of statements where one statement is related to another and never acquires an absolute point to base itself on. This might be called a skepticism in terms of *validity* or *certainty* of historical knowledge, as against the former in terms of the object. Actually the skepticism in terms of the object is the source of the skepticism in terms of validity. Were it possible to step across the boundaries of knowledge and reach the facts

---

[25] *Ibid.*
[26] *Ibid.*, p. 214.
[27] *Ibid.*, p. 216.
[28] *Ibid.*, p. 217.

as they really were, then it would also be possible to break out of the quasi-self-contained network of statement.

We may indeed restate in this context, *"Beim ersten sind wir frei."* Once we decide to go on with historical knowledge, we decide not to be concerned with the happenings in the past but with what is present. This decision makes historical knowledge fully possible, since it determines the interest of this knowledge. We no longer consider this to be a shortcoming of historical knowledge, as it can be considered from the outside, or before the very beginning; on the contrary, this is its very nature, once it is considered from within. There is a point at which we brush aside the perpetual doubt (interestingly enough Collingwood sees here an affinity between science and philosophy, since both are free to question everything)[29] and assume something. This assumption turns out to be the resting-point of historical knowledge, that is to say, that evidence which historical knowledge looks for: "It thus appears that history is not doubtful at all. It seemed doubtful, to say the least, so long as we imagined its object to be the past as past."[30] To sum up we may say: reliance on evidence is at once the shortcoming of historical knowledge and its very nature. "The historian does not first think of a problem and then search for evidence bearing on it, it is his possession of evidence bearing on a problem that alone makes the problem a real one."[31] The evidence is the basis for historical knowledge and that driving force for the actual piece of historical research, as an *Anstoss* in the Neo-Kantian sense of the word, without assuming any historical connection between Collingwood and the Neo-Kantian school.

If we look closer at this view of the relation between historical knowledge and the datum which has the function of evidence, we find the line of argument which has been put forward in *Speculum Mentis* as to the nature of history. History supersedes science in the dialectical and historical development of Mind, since there is no way of assuming an infinite regression of suppositions, and science is a thinking in suppositions. The ladder of suppositions has to be terminated and thus end up in facts, which in turn are the concern of history. The freedom to doubt everything which is characteristic of science, is nothing but an infinite regression of suppositions, as envisaged in *Speculum Mentis*, while the reliance on a datum is a reformulation of the relation of his-

---

[29] Cf. *ibid.*
[30] *Ibid.*, p. 222.
[31] *Ibid.*

tory to facts. The logic of the argument has not changed, only its realm has changed: there are no facts, but data, that is to say, facts within the scope of knowledge lacking any independent existence outside it.

b) To rely on evidence, in spite of the immanent skepticism that is tied up with the very nature of this evidence, is an act of decision; it is an act of the historian. The freedom of the historian becomes manifest in his decision to run the risk inherent in his reliance upon evidence and still to go on with his pursuit. Collingwood did not formulate the decision of the historian as an act of freedom; he preferred to call it an *irrational* act. But we may formulate his view in terms of the historian's freedom, since later he came to see the problem of the historian's freedom as prominent, and in a way as the central problem of his doctrine. The introduction of imagination as the means of historical cognition already points to the freedom of the historian, since imagination is a free manifestation of the mental capacities of the historian. The same issue comes to the fore in the relation of the historian to the datum, and this problem is only the other side of the same coin.

The well-known criticism of "scissors and paste history" is yet another indication of the struggle to provide for the freedom of the historian, although, as we shall have to show, a restricted freedom. "Instead of repeating statements accepted on the testimony of authorities, the historian of today makes his own statements on his own authority according to what he finds the evidence in his possession to prove when he analyses it with a certain question in his mind."[32] The characteristic expressions in this context, which underline the freedom of the historian towards the world he is exploring, are "the authority of the historian" and the "question in his mind." The historian does not accept any given evidence; he approaches the datum with a question in his own mind. One may suggest here a terminological distinction, although it is not made by Collingwood himself, between the historical *datum* and historical *evidence*. The historian approaches the datum with a question in his mind and thus challenges the datum to answer his question. This is the "Baconian sense of history," or one might say, the Kantian feature in Collingwood's system, where one does not face nature as a pupil but as a judge who asks nature suitable questions.[33] There is a considerable amount of freedom on the part of the historian according to that view, since the historian imposes on the datum a

[32] *An Essay on Metaphysics*, p. 59.
[33] Cf. *Critique of Pure Reason*, B. XIII, (N. Kemp-Smith's translation, London 1950 p. 20).

meaningful framework which is not of the datum as such. Yet this freedom is restricted, since historical research is carried out in a sort of interplay between the datum and the historian, or in a sort of interdependence of the two. In a rough paraphrase of Kant's formula we may say that data without questions would be blind, while questions without data would be empty. Collingwood himself sums up this interdependence of the two factors: "people did not understand that history is a kind of thinking whereby absolutely cogent inferences about the past are drawn from interpretations of the evidence it has left behind".[34] Freedom is freedom of decision to start with historical knowledge. The content of this knowledge is provided by the datum and by the historian himself. This freedom, moreover, increases; the historian, through "the question in his mind," is co-responsible for the meaning of the historical evidence. With the increasing emphasis placed on the freedom of the historian, the validity of the historical picture becomes guaranteed. We have been shown before that to the degree that history is tied to an object outside knowledge, the historical picture can never be certain. Hence, since historical knowledge has freed itself from its chains, there is less room for skepticism in terms of the validity of its statements. It is not by chance that Collingwood now refers to history and its inferences as "absolutely cogent inferences." Or in another formulation: "History had by now established itself as a science, that is a progressive inquiry in which conclusions are solidly and demonstratively established."[35] This is again a paradoxical feature in Collingwood's system: the more historical knowledge relies on data, the more uncertain it is. The more history relies on the freedom of the historian, the more it becomes certain in its statements and conclusions. This "Copernican turn" in Collingwood's system is remarkable on its own merits, since it shows the hidden epistemological consideration as a driving force for the re-shaping of its view. It seems as if Collingwood refused to be satisfied with the irrational decision to accept the foundations of historical knowledge and strove to lay down a new foundation for them. Collingwood appears here, as it were, as following both Hume and Kant: he first overcame the skepticism inherent in historical knowledge by a kind of "belief" which cuts off the skeptical structure; he then carried out the "Copernican turn" which made historical knowledge revolve around the historian, and thus considered it justifiable to attribute certainty to historical findings. This is not to say that the

---

[34] *An Essay on Metaphysics*, p. 58.
[35] *The Idea of Nature*, Oxford, 1945, p. 13.

epistemological consideration was the only motive for this progressive emancipation of the historian from the bonds of evidence. But this was one of the motives, even one of the main ones. Once Collingwood set out on this way, he necessarily had to wrestle with the problem of how to avoid the danger of emptiness in history, that is to say, how to avoid the danger that, with the establishment of the freedom of the historian, the *object* of history would disappear altogether: the historian's picture would be full and certain but might turn out to be fictitious. Here again we face the problem of the similarity and the difference between a piece of historical research and an historical novel, a similarity already mentioned in connection with the position of imagination in history. Collingwood faced at this point the danger expressed in Kant's well-known simile: "The light dove, cleaving the air in her free flight, and feeling its resistance, might imagine that its flight would be still easier in empty space."[36]

The main step towards the emancipation of the historian from the chains of the datum was made by transferring the datum to the realm of the present, i.e. to the dimension inhabited by the historian himself. Towards the datum located in his own realm, the historian assumes in the first place an attitude of questioning. But Collingwood went a step further: once we assume the importance of the evidence, though it is evidence within the realm of the historian, we still assume a tension within the world of the historian: that between his own impetus and the given evidence. There is no place in Collingwood's system where he is so eager to overcome all tension and to show history to be harmonious, as in this part of dealing with the position of the datum in historical knowledge. "The freedom that there is in history," he writes, "consists in the fact that this compulsion is imposed upon the activity of human reason not by anything else, but by itself,"[37] and "the historian discovers the autonomous character of historical thought, its power to solve its own problems for itself by its own methods."[38] "History is its own criterion; it does not depend for its validity on something outside itself, it is an autonomous form of thought with its own principles and its own methods."[39] This last statement seems to be very clear in its tendency to establish the autarky of historical knowledge. The expression "something outside itself" may refer to the datum which is in a way superimposed on historical knowledge. This will be the radical inter-

[36] *Critique of Pure Reason*, B 9, (ed. cited, p. 47).
[37] *The Idea of History*, p. 317.
[38] *Ibid.*, p. 318.
[39] *Ibid.*, p. 140.

pretation of Collingwood's statement, which is reinforced time and
again by his various expressions to the effect that the historian is master
in his own house.[40] Collingwood himself did not interpret this statement
in a milder form, i.e., that since evidence is located in the present, it is inside historical knowledge, and historical knowledge is therefore independent of any outside factor. The milder interpretation of this statement
would fit what Collingwood said before, in the early phases of his system.
Actually Collingwood was very fond of emphasizing the radical meaning
of his statement, in order fully to connect the historical picture or conclusion with the historical consciousness itself. Every dependence on
a piece of evidence seemed to be a kind of dogmatic-realistic history.
The datum or the evidence was understood as "raw material" which
cannot be a guiding principle in establishing the historical truth. And
yet, once Collingwood reached the radical conclusion of his own system, he hesitated to maintain it because he was aware of the possibility of obliterating any border line that might separate history from
the historical novel. And there is no other way to establish this border
line unless we retain the despised datum or evidence.

There is one radical expression in Collingwood's usage which presents the objective of his system, and which conceives of history in
Cartesian language as an "innate idea," or in Kantian language as
a priori.[41] When one analyses this expression one wonders what it
actually connotes: does Collingwood assume that the actual, fragmentary historical picture as given by Gibbon, Ranke or Acton is an innate
idea or an a priori concept, or does he mean to say that the historical
trend in the consciousness, the fact that consciousness looks at the
world sub specie historiae, is a feature of consciousness as such, which
cannot be derived from any given evidence or from any encountered
datum? The historical interest of the consciousness precedes from this
point of view any piece of historical research and thus may be called
a priori. But precisely because consciousness has in itself the immanent
historical impulse, it needs evidence or it needs a datum in order to ac-
tivate its "innate" interest. The historical perspective would be empty
without the datum. It seems that when Collingwood introduced into his
vocabulary the traditional terminology of the innate idea or of the a
priori, he was not aware of the difference between the two aspects in
history, and he assumed that even the historical picture of a period or a
trend (and not only the historical trend as such), is a priori or innate. It

40 Cf. ibid., p. 155.
41 Ibid., p. 247.

is an assumption similar to one which asserts not only the principle of causality to be *a priori*, but also the explanation of the rain falling in the winter of 1950 as an *a priori* statement. The radical transfer of history from that which depends upon a datum to that which is fully autonomous may be parallel to some trends in modern science – as represented e.g. by Eddington – which abolish the distinction between *a priori* principles and material laws along with the concrete statements embodying these laws. But this trend must be criticized in history even more than in science, since the datum in history is one in a given dimension of time, that is to say, in the present, and as such cannot be obliterated.

Actually the programme formulated by Collingwood is more radical than the examples he introduced to prove it. "Far from relying on an authority other than himself, to whose statements his thought must conform, the historian is his own authority and his thought autonomous, self-authorising, possessed of a criterion to which his so-called authorities must conform and by reference to which they are criticized."[42] But the examples introduced are of selection and interpretation in historical research; in other words, they illustrate the fact that the historian does not deal with everything which is present in his world but constructs a picture out of what is present by introducing links of connection which are not present. Yet, precisely because there is this kind of activity on the part of the historian, we must realize that this is an activity exercised with reference to a datum, which is interpreted through interpolation and is constructed through selection. The freedom of the historian is exercised in relation to the superimposed datum and not in a vacuum.

In the early system, the startingpoint for historical research was in evidence. The position of the evidence was well-established even when it was understood as a mere *Anstoss*, to use the Neo-Kantian term once again. Once the shift is made towards the historian, there is no fixed position left to the evidence. "In scientific history anything is evidence which is used as evidence, and no one can know what is going to be useful as evidence until he has had occasion to use it,"[43] and "everything in the world is potential evidence for any subject whatever."[44] The same idea is expressed in a different way with a clear reference to the datum: in history, "just as there are, properly speaking,

[42] *Ibid.*, p. 236.
[43] *Ibid.*, p. 280.
[44] *Ibid.*

no authorities, so there are, properly speaking, no data."[45] And "when we ask what gives historical thought this datum, the answer is obvious: historical thought gives it to itself, and therefore in relation to historical thought at large it is not a datum but a result or achievement. It is only our historical knowledge which tells us ... that the passage is authentic Thucydides, not an interpolation or corruption."[46] Here again Collingwood's close affinity to the Marburg School in German philosophy reveals itself, even in the terminology he used: the datum is not given, it is an achievement. This expression corresponds to the distinction made by the Marburg School between *gegeben* and *aufgegeben*, though biographically speaking one cannot assume any actual relation of Collingwood with the Marburg School of Hermann Cohen and Paul Natorp. Collingwood made here a very important observation about the nature of the historical datum. The datum is itself included in the historical universe of discourse and does not occupy an independent position outside it. But we have to ask ourselves whether we are entitled to formulate this idea in as radical a fashion as Collingwood did. It seems that within the concept of the datum Collingwood did not distinguish between the datum proper and the meaning of it. The meaning is certainly attributed, established, and proved by historical knowledge. But the meaning is *attached* or attributed to something which has a position not only within the scope of historical consciousness but also *vis-à-vis* this consciousness, as for instance the text of Thucydides. Knowledge attributes meanings but does not create the co-ordinates or substrata of meanings. These are given, and as such they demand their acknowledgement by knowledge, and as such they give knowledge the momentum for their exploration and explanation. In the mood of over-hasty idealism, Collingwood tended, in accordance with the Italian pattern, to interpret mind and knowledge as pure act, and thus annihilated the intrinsic polarity of all knowledge, including historical knowledge.

Let us also examine critically the statement that in history everything can be evidence. This could only be affirmed so long as Collingwood did not take into account the time factor in history. In what sense can the fact, for instance, that there was a French Revolution in 1789 prove that there had been the Glorious Revolution of 1688? One might say that the French Revolution was an outcome of the transplantation of revolutionary ideas from the British Isles to the Continent and that there would have been no French Revolution unless

---

[45] *Ibid.*, p. 243.
[46] *Ibid.*, p. 244.

there had previously been the Glorious Revolution. But this cannot be considered as evidence, since evidence must have, among other things, a closer connection with the investigated fact or event, and a closer connection is very often one in terms of time, as for instance, evidence contemporaneous with the event, derived from an actual observer, from memoirs, documents, etc. This can be shown in an example from Biblical history: why do we look for "independent evidence," that is to say for sources which are not in the Bible itself, in order to establish or ascertain the historical truth of the events as recounted in the Bible? We may not be satisfied with the kind of evidence which is embodied in the Scriptures themselves, or in the living tradition related to the Scriptures. The fact that a sage of the second century of our era held the stories to be reliable, is not historical evidence for the truth of the stories as such, but evidence only for the continuity of thought or belief throughout the generations. Had, however, a sage of the tenth century B.C. related independently one of the stories included in the Bible, that would be evidence, at least supplementary evidence. This indicates that not everything is evidence, and that there are some methodological and common-sense limitations for the use of what may constitute historical evidence. The historian is not free entirely with reference to the evidence he faces, and not everything is evidence because of its usefulness. Sometimes, indeed, the reverse might be true; since it is useful it has to be handled with caution; being useful may sometimes support wishful thinking. Now, there is a compulsion exercised on the mind of the historian by the meaning of his subject-matter, and hence the freedom and the autonomy of the historian are of necessity restricted. Historical knowledge is a dialectial encounter between the determinability of the datum and the determination attributed by consciousness. Any attempt to do away with this encounter and make historical knowledge unilateral, as Collingwood's extreme view does, is bound to fail.

In terms of Collingwood's own development, we may sum up the phases of his system by saying that what was considered before as the ground for skepticism about historical knowledge becomes the cornerstone for the new structure of history. That there is in history no definite evidence, that on the contrary, history is a self-sustaining network of evidence – here is the real advantage in looking at history from the point of view of philosophy: historical knowledge demonstrates the independence of mind. But the critical question still remains, whether both partners, history and philosophy, profit from this *rapprochement* or whether this *rapprochement* is not forced, carried out against the best and legitimate interest of the two partners involved.

3. *Time*

a) Collingwood is a unique example of a philosopher of history who did not "take time seriously." We have to consider now whether a view which does not regard the time-factor as essential in history, can be a legitimate one or not. One thing is clear: a serious attempt has been made in this direction, and hence any view which stresses the central position of the time-factor in history must overcome the challenge implied in Collingwood's attempt.

We could think that Collingwood's neglect of the time-factor in history is connected with the view of the identity of history and philosophy dealt with before. The placing of history on the plane of philosophy necessarily involves the viewing of historical contents *sub specie aeternitatis*. But in point of fact this is not what Collingwood does: the consideration of the time-factor in history as secondary already appears in *Speculum Mentis*, and that is a work which explicitly insists on a clear distinction between philosophy and history. Therefore the factor which determined Collingwood's view must lie elsewhere, though the relationship to philosophy has some bearing here as well.

There is a passage in *Speculum Mentis* which is worth detailed analysis.

> ... the reader may have imagined that when we spoke of the process of thought we were presupposing the reality of time, since every process is a process in time. Hence time would appear to be something external to the absolute mind, the necessity which stands over Zeus himself. But so to regard time is to forget that the process of which we are speaking is a process not of mechanical change but of thought: a self-knowing process. A mind which knows its own change is by that very knowledge lifted above change. History – and the same is true of memory and even perception – is the mind's triumph over time. ... All concrete thought is, in its immediacy, temporal, but in its mediation extemporal. The mind in its actual thinking at once recognizes and defies temporal (and spatial) limitations. ... Time is not a mere appearance; it is perfectly real; but like all opposites it can be real only as the correlative of its equally real opposite, eternity.[47]

(1) Let us, in the first place, draw attention to the Hegelian motifs included in this view: the process of the manifestation of mind Collingwood is considering is conceived in Hegelian terms, i.e. it is not a process in time, but one of self-knowing, the latter being eventually extratemporal. What is equally Hegelian is the notion that to know something is to be beyond the realm of that known object.

(2) Collingwood points here to a non-Newtonian conception of time:

---

[47] *Speculum Mentis*, pp. 300–301.

time is not an external and absolute framework within which the process occurs. Time is a part of the content itself, and with the dialectical change of the content the time-factor changes as well. To put it in other words: time itself changes, but things or events do not change in time. The question which is raised by this view is: Where does time change, if time itself is involved in the dialectical process of change? Collingwood takes a radical view: it would be pointless to assume that time changes within what still is time. Time changes within something which is above time, i.e. eternity.

(3) Eternity however is not understood here in religious or Platonic terms. It is not an idea which is placed above time, neither is it the divine essence. It is knowledge itself which overcomes time. Collingwood does not point to the *act of knowledge*, which is a temporal occasion in its immediacy, as he calls it, again in Hegelian terms. Only the *content* of knowledge is a-temporal. In every act of cognition there is to be found this eternal element of content. All cognition is related to a *Wahrheit an sich*, if we may use here Bolzano's expression. In all cognition we are related to time, since we conceive something existent. At the same time, however, we are raised to an a-temporal plane, since we release the content of our knowledge from its interfusion with reality. If knowledge were a process only, it would belong to the realm of reality and therefore be confined to time. But since knowledge has a content, since it possesses the ideal element in itself, it defies time.

(4) Time is a dialectical concept, and therefore must intrinsically point to its opposite, viz. to eternity. It is meaningful to describe something as being in time only from a perspective outside time. Thus there is a clear distinction: time and facts on the one hand, and knowledge of facts and eternity on the other.

We may now realize what lies behind Collingwood's radical view: the essence of knowledge is seen beyond and above time, because knowledge transforms reality into thought. The question which Collingwood did not raise is: Why should this defiance of time be a particular feature of history? Why does it appear only with the manifestation of mind *qua* history? If the overcoming of time by its transformation into thought is responsible for the a-temporal character of thought, then, at the very least the same process is to be found in science. In science, too, mind does not dwell in the realm of the reality existing in time. Moreover, the abstract or hypothetical nature of science displays in its relation to facts the power of mind, perhaps even more than does history. If thought as such provides for the a-temporal character of the realm of history, then there would be, from this point of view, no difference between history and science. The whole dialectical structure of the system would be one of two realms: mind *qua* reality and bound with time, on the one hand, and mind *qua* a-temporal activity, on the other. This dualism would hardly fit the monistic trend of the system as expressed in *Speculum Mentis*.

And further: Collingwood assumes that the antithesis of time is eternity. He is certainly right in terms of the history of ideas, both in metaphysics and in religion. He looks, as it were, for an ontological antithesis for time; he looks for something which would be real, but not in the sense of the reality of the facts. This, however, is a dogmatic-ontological presupposition: against the antithesis between time and eternity one may legitimately posit a difference between time and the principles of understanding time, seeing that these principles are neither eternal in the ontological sense, nor real in the sense of factual reality. The principle of causality admittedly refers to reality and has a function in relation; but is it an element of reality in the sense that events are? Or, to take another and nearer example, is time as a form of knowledge, in Kant's sense, a reality in time, or is it, in Collingwood's sense, an eternity, or an element in the realm of eternity? Time in Kant's sense is neither the one nor the other, since it is a form or a principle of knowledge which masters knowledge and the facts referred to in knowledge, but it is still not inheriting a particular ontological sphere of its own.

Thirdly: Collingwood himself taught in the later phases of his system that historical knowledge starts with the present. It is not only that the object of historical knowledge is one in time, but also that knowledge itself is referred to time. Are we to consider the relation of knowledge to the present, i.e. to a particular dimension of time, as one belonging to the immediate aspect of knowledge as a sheer act and hence to be overcome in the mediated aspect, viz. in thought? It seems that the present is referred to as more than only a factor which stimulates historical knowledge or activates it and is thus merely an external element of knowledge. The relation to the present shapes the actual content of knowledge, and no one was more eager than Collingwood to point out this feature of historical knowledge. It might be considered unfair to criticize the early views of Collingwood by taking advantage of the concepts he provided later. This, however, is a different criticism whose objective is only to stress that it is precisely historical knowledge which does not allow this identification of thought with the over-

coming of time. Such identification would be characteristic rather of
scientific (natural) knowledge, for there it is irrelevant "when" and
"where" the knowledge takes place; conversely, the "when" and
"where" of historical knowledge is a matter of considerable importance.

b) The implicit notion that thought means overcoming time was persistent with Collingwood; it remained an integral part of his system
even after his outlook on the nature of history had changed quite
radically. Thought was responsible for overcoming time when the object of history was considered to be simply a fact; thought is all the
more the factor responsible for the overcoming of time when precisely
thought itself becomes the object of history. In the system of *Speculum
Mentis* the thought of the historian alone resulted in the overcoming of
time, while in the mature system of the *Autobiography* and *The Idea
of History* both the object and the subject of history are united in
thought, which in turn is the factor which defies time.

Collingwood states this view in negative terms by saying that change
and history are not at all the same.[48] He tries to free the notion of history from the notion of processes in time, as it is usually conceived. But
he states his views just as clearly in positive terms: "The peculiarity
which makes it historical is not the fact of its happening in time, but
the fact of its becoming known to us by our re-thinking the same
thought which created the situation we are investigating, and thus
coming to understand that situation."[49] History is not defined through
its subject-matter but through its way of cognition – this is the view
that was earlier referred to as the Copernican turn in Collingwood's
system. Now, the Copernican turn carries with it an important conclusion with regard to the background of time in history; thought is
re-thought, in spite of the difference between the past and the present.
Thus thought is in a way indifferent to the distinction in terms of the
dimensions of time. Historical knowledge is altogether possible because in that knowledge we defy time and bring about a meeting of
thoughts which are above time. The meeting itself seems to be above
time, since it takes place in the realm of thought. To put the view in
other terms: history is possible since time is defied.

What led Collingwood to state his view in such an extreme form?
Apparently he intended to re-formulate the possibility of permanence
in history as explained by T. M. Knox. Historicism defies all perma-

[48] Cf. *The Idea of History*, p. 210.
[49] *Ibid.*, p. 218.

nence in history, turning every event into something transitional only; Collingwood wants to show that history is immanently connected with an anti-historicist presupposition, since history is possible, or historical understanding is meaningful, only if and when the event *qua* thought is re-thought at a time subsequent to its actual occurrence. Thus re-thinking provides for the continuity of history and makes historical occasion universal, as Collingwood himself calls it. Actually, Collingwood moderates his former view: there is no longer the antithesis of *time and eternity* but the antithesis of *transience and permanence,* and he seems to consider permanence to be defiance of time. In this sense history is not concerned with events in time and the time-factor in history is a secondary one, at the most. History itself overcomes historicism by overcoming time. (See the above analysis of Collingwood's historicism.) This is a very adventurous step in the philosophy of history, but it seems doubtful whether one can "save the phenomena" by means of this device. Three points should be stressed in the present context:

(1) Eternity is the antithesis of time, but permanence is not. Permanence has a meaning precisely in terms of time; something is permanent not out of time but inside time, as was shown in Kant's First Analogy of Experience. Permanence is the antithesis of *transience,* but not the antithesis of *time;* the permanent is permanent in time and not outside it.

(2) There is a kind of *pars pro toto* fallacy in Collingwood's argument: he succeeds in showing that in historical knowledge the gap between the past and the present is bridged. But the bridging of the difference between the time-*dimensions* does not connote the defiance of *time,* since the defiance of the gap between the time-dimensions is not at all an annihilation of time. Re-enactment of thought occurs *after* the thinking of the original thought, precisely because it is the former which is engaged in re-enacting. In spite of the meeting in the realm of thought, the feature of succession which is an essential feature of time, holds good. *The defiance of the time-gap takes place in time,* and we have to stress here both the *taking place* which points to the fact that this itself is an occasion, and *time,* which points to the fact that the time-factor is the background even of the annihilation of the time-gap.

(3) Finally, the meeting between past thought and present thought through re-enactment presupposes awareness of the fact that it is precisely *past thought* which is being re-enacted. The meeting itself occurs within one historical dimension, the dimension of the present.

The time-gap is bridged through the activity of one of the time-dimensions, i.e. the dimension of the present. Defiance of time amounts only to the defiance of the past by the present. This indeed is significant in terms of an epistemology of history, but this does not elevate history into a realm which is above time altogether. The epistemology of history analyses historical knowledge in its real essence, and thus discovers the essential connection of historical knowledge with time.

In a way Collingwood is able to conceal this essence of historical knowledge since, in place of the distinction between the time-dimensions of past and present, the epistemological distinction between the object (past thought) and the subject (present thought in the mind of the historian) is put forward. But the epistemological equivalent of the time-dimensions is at the most no more than an isomorphic translation of these dimensions. Both the object and the subject have an epistemological meaning because of their being involved in time, and not because of their intrinsic epistemological status. The epistemological status is only an expression of their status in time. Thus time has not been overcome in Collingwood's system; on the contrary, it has been re-emphasized.

c) This concentration on the dimension of the present points to a further motif in Collingwood's theory of the antithetical relation of history and time. A paper dated 1925,[50] though not dealing exclusively with the problem of time in history, throws light on this particular problem. Collingwood distinguished there between the real and the ideal: the present alone is real, while both the past and the future are ideal. The past is ideal in *modo necessitatis* whereas the future is ideal in *modo possibilitatis*.

What is significant – in the context of the philosophy of history – is the tendency to translate the time-dimensions into modal distinctions, and thus to abolish the primary and irreducible nature of time. Collingwood does not want to make time illusory and therefore stresses that time is transcendentally real and thus the logical presupposition of any thought whatever.[51] But in spite of this status of time, time in its dimensions has a clear equivalent in the modal differences.

The fact that only the dimension of the present is real as against the ideality of the other time dimensions certainly has a bearing on the

---

[50] "Some Perplexities about Time", *Proceedings of the Aristotelian Society*, Vol. XXVI, London, 1925–1926, pp. 135–150.
[51] Cf. *ibid.*, p. 150.

problem of time in history "but this does not mean that the past *as
past* continues to exist. What does continue to exist is the contribution
it has made to the present."[52] Thus the present is the real focus of time
and history, and this is in accord with the view propounded in the later
writings.

There is no need to dwell on the attempt to transform the meaning
of the time-dimensions into modal differences, nor to discuss here in
what sense it is true that the modal equivalent of the past is necessity,
while that of the future is possibility.[53] The main point for the discussion of the position of time in history is Collingwood's assumption
that time has actually a decisive ontological power: it is time that
transmutes reality into ideality and again ideality into reality. What
has been present becomes past and thus what has been real becomes
ideal *in time* and through *the passage of time*. The same is to be applied
to the future, since time and the passage of time turn the future, which
is ideal only from the point of view of the *present present*, into a reality
from the point of view of the *future present*. Actually it is *time* that
creates the modal differences. Collingwood wanted to transform the
time differences into modal ones without realizing, it seems, that it is
precisely time that makes this transformation possible. Moreover, time
has a creative power in relation to what has been considered to be
elevated above time, viz. the realm of ideality. Ideality is not a conceptual antithesis of time and reality; it is created by time itself. Hence
– according to this view – it is ideality which is defied, and not time. We
may say that Collingwood does not get rid of time as he wished, that
he retains time and even increases its relevance in spite of himself and
of his general tendency not to take it seriously. It is therefore by no
means accidental that every once in a while Collingwood returns
explicitly to the position of time in history. We have to deal with this
reverse side of his system.

d) Even in his late system, where the defiance of time is stressed so
much, Collingwood feels himself compelled, as it were, to point to the
time-factor in history, that is to say, to consider history as a process in
spite of its being the meeting of past and present thought. The essence
of history "lies not in its consisting of individual facts, however valu-
able these facts may be, but in the process of development leading from

---

[52] *Ibid.*, p. 144.
[53] The present author has discussed this question in *Between Past and Present, An Essay
on History*, pp. 112ff.

one to another."[54] Moreover, Collingwood sees the impact of history on science in the fact that the notion of process has penetrated science. "The historical conception of scientifically knowable change or process was applied, under the name of evolution, to the natural world,"[55] and "the tendency to resolve the very ancient dualism between changing and unchanging elements in the world of nature by maintaining that what had hitherto been regarded as unchanging was itself in reality subject to change ... the origin of this tendency ... must be sought in the historical movement of the late eighteenth century."[56] Thus history is explicitly identified with process, although process does not mean only destroying, but creating as well.[57] Both destroying and creating are manifestations of the general character of history in which *tout casse, tout lasse, tout passe*.[58] There is no problem here of the overcoming of the process in time in history, which is the main point in Collingwood's system. This indicates Collingwood's oscillation between his main trend and his tendency to take refuge in the common-sense meaning of history *qua* process. Within the structure of Collingwood's system, the understanding of history as a process of change which takes place in time, is systematically expressed in his conception of the nature of metaphysics. This is a clear expression of the historicist trend in Collingwood's system, which trend once again is related to the status of time in history. "Questions as to what absolute presuppositions have been made on certain occasions. This was not an accident. All metaphysical questions are historical questions, and all metaphysical propositions are historical propositions."[59] Historical questions are questions about thought which occur on particular occasions. They are changing questions and along with them the metaphysical systems change as well. There are no eternal questions in the realm of ideality, removed from the reality of time. There is no distinction between ideality and reality, and thought is placed within reality and hence within time. History is related to time.

Here again there is a kind of regression in Collingwood's system which brings him back to the realm of time. In conclusion, we may say that Collingwood oscillates between two polar views of history: on the one hand, he wants to save history from the – as it were – destroying

[54] *The Idea of History*, p. 169.
[55] *The Idea of Nature*, p. 10.
[56] *Ibid.*
[57] Cf. *ibid.*, p. 27.
[58] Cf. *An Essay of Metaphysics*, p. 74.
[59] *Ibid.*, p. 49.

activity of time and thus overcome historicism. On the other hand, he stresses the process in history; and here he is an historicist. Collingwood implies that there is only one possibility: either time and historicism, or else defiance of time and hence the removal of the very foundation on which historicism stands.

What is lacking in Collingwood is a synthesis based on an analysis of historical time, a synthesis that is beyond the generic concept of process and yet is more than the sheer contraction of time in history to the dimension of the present. Collingwood leaves us with respect to time either in the realm above time or in the realm below *historical* time, historical time being conceived as a particular set of relations between the time-dimensions, and as specific to the realm of history. This is one of the main shortcomings of his approach to history.

4. *Science* versus *History*

a) The issue of the difference between scientific and historical knowledge with reference to the problem of individuality *versus* generality, has been broached in modern philosophy as the main trait differentiating the two branches of knowledge. In the first phase of his system, Collingwood shares this view of the difference between science and history. He holds that the main feature of science is abstractness; that science uses general concepts which are indifferent to the variations of the particulars.[60] The abstractness of science connotes generality. Or to put it differently, Collingwood adheres to the empiricist view of the nature of concepts: he assumes that concepts are general since they are abstract. Facts as such are concrete and thus individual. Science removes from the nature of the facts their individuality and turns *individuals* into *particulars* to be classified in classes and to be considered as examples of something general:[61] "scientific fact is a fact purged of its crude and scientifically scandalous concreteness, isolated from its historical setting and reduced to the status of a mere instance of a rule."[62] The dogmatic nature of this assumption lies in the combination of the notion of abstractness with the notion of generality. Therefore Collingwood sees the dichotomy between facts and rules as one between instances and rules. He does not consider the possibility of looking at individual occurrences as at *specifications* of the principles.

[60] See *Speculum Mentis*, p. 186.
[61] *Ibid.*
[62] *Ibid.*

This latter view would be different from the naïve view, which Colling-wood seems to share, that individual occasions are given and hence are artificially overcome in the process of scientific abstraction. In the later phase of his thought, he did not change his view of the nature of science in terms of its usage of general concepts, but he did change his view as to the nature of the individuality dealt with in history. He enhanced the meaning of individuality, which he had taken in the first place as no more than given, factual and thus merely encountered by knowledge.

b) The first step taken towards a new understanding of the relation between science and history was one which abolished the former clear-cut distinction.[63] This change has a certain epistemological, or at least methodological, background. The understanding of the various forms of mind is based on the analysis of their position within the total system of manifestations of mind. Each form is considered radically in its nature; each form is considered to be complete in itself as a particular and partial form. However, since it is particular and partial, it turns dialectically into the next form and is replaced by the next one in the scheme of forms. The epistemological outlook as stated in the paper of 1922 is different: Collingwood does not explicitly approach the various forms involved, i.e. science and history, as complete and rounded in themselves. He is concerned with the ways of obtaining scientific and historical knowledge respectively. In terms of the nature of the methodological approach, the dichotomy of science and history disappears, and the "distinction between them as separate kinds of knowledge is an illusion,"[64] based more on the historical origins of the two kinds of knowledge, than on reasons inherent in principles. There are three points which science and history may be shown to have in common, the first of which has already been mentioned, namely the relation between the general and the individual.

(1) "To be a chemist consists not in knowing the general formulae but in interpreting particular changes which we observe taking place by means of these formulae. ... even mathematics does not consist of abstract equations and formulae but in the application of these to the interpretation of our own mathematical operations."[65] In contrast

---

[63] Actually the article which considers the similarity of the two kinds of knowledge is earlier than the book which sees them as different.

[64] "Are History and Science Different Kinds of Knowledge?" (A Symposium by R. G. Collingwood, A. E .Taylor, and F. C. S. Schiller), *Mind*, Vol. XXXI/124, 1922, I, p. 450.

[65] *Ibid.*, p. 447.

with the former view where the realm of general concepts was considered to be independent and isolated and clearly distinguished from that
of individual instances, the new view stresses the methodological value
of the general concept. The general concept is a means towards the
understanding of the individual facts. The main problem implied in
the scientific concepts is their applicability, that is to say, their validity
for individual facts. Since there is an inherent connection between the
general and the individual, there is an affinity between science, which
is interested in the general, and history which is interested in the individual, as Collingwood himself pointed out in the previous discussion.
It is proper to observe that Collingwood does not come back to the
distinction between the individual and the particular, and does not
raise the question whether the individual, as conceived in terms of the
concepts employed by science, does not cease to be an individual and
becomes merely a particular.[66]

(2) Neither is the distinction between science and history – according
to their relation to time-dimensions – a valid one. To say simply that
history deals with the past while science is naturally indifferent to
time-dimensions, obliges one to face the problem that geology, for
instance, which is a scientific discipline, deals with the past, as history
does.[67] Admittedly, Collingwood is not concerned here with the problem of the difference between the past dealt with in geology, and that
dealt with in history, that is to say, the difference between them arising
from the fact that geology deals with occurrences in the "macro-time"
of the earth while history deals with occurrences in the "micro-time"
of human beings. Further, and still more important: the strata of the
earth do not get to know themselves in geology, in contradistinction
to history where the active human beings get to know themselves
through historical knowledge. To put it in Collingwood's own terms:
there is no room for re-enactment in the realm of geology, whereas the
realm of history presupposes an act of re-enactment, an act which in
turn presupposes the identity of the subject and the object in history,
of the knower and the known. Collingwood does not make any of these
observations in this context.

A further significant observation in terms of the relation of both
science and history to time-dimensions, is made in connection with the
place of prediction in history. "History predicts that green glaze pot-

---

[66] Compare the statement in *Speculum Mentis*, p. 199: "the quarrel between history and
science is whether generalization is a means to knowledge or knowledge itself".
[67] Cf. *ibid.*, p. 450.

tery will be found in medieval ruins."[68] To be sure, Collingwood disregards here – and very significantly so, from his own point of view as to the position of time in history – the difference between two kinds of predictions: a prediction directed towards events in the future which have not yet occurred, and a prediction concerned with the nature of events and their traces which have already occurred, but have not as yet been discovered, as for instance pottery which was manufactured in the Middle Ages but has not yet been unearthed. Collingwood may disregard this difference between the two kinds of prediction since for him what is unknown is non-existent: being undiscovered, the pottery is unknown, and hence non-existent. It occupies epistemologically the same position as is occupied by the non-existent future event in time. The epistemologically non-existent fact is – for him – tantamount to the ontologically non-existent fact. Therefore Collingwood can consistently assume that there is a prediction in history as well. But even if we must reject this view because of the confusion of the two kinds of prediction – a view which ultimately originates from a disregard for the time-factor in history – the importance of his observation still holds good: actually what Collingwood pointed out is the methodological similarity between *prediction* on the one hand and *hypothetical thinking* on the other. The assumption that green glaze pottery will be unearthed is actually an hypothetical assumption. As an hypothesis it is an anticipation of facts; prediction of a future event is also the anticipation of a fact. From this point of view there is a real affinity between the methodological nature of hypothesis and the nature of prediction. Yet a prediction is an anticipation of events which have not yet occurred, while an historical hypothesis is the anticipation of an event unknown within the realm of the *historian*, and not one which has not as yet occurred. An historical hypothesis is the anticipation of an event to be *encountered* by the historian and not of an event due to occur. The fact that historical knowledge makes use of hypotheses may be at variance with another of Collingwood's views concerning the categorical nature of historical knowledge on the one hand, and the hypothetical nature of scientific knowledge on the other – a view expounded in *Speculum Mentis*. In spite of this, it is clearly shown by Collingwood himself, in the observation quoted, that historical knowledge needs hypotheses and actually uses them.

(3) The affinity between science and history is to be found in a third common feature: history and science are both interpretations. It could

[68] *Ibid.*

be argued that the very abstractness of science of itself involves interpretation. From this point of view there is nothing new in the emphasis
on the nature of science as interpretation. Yet the term itself is new
and significant, since it is usually associated with historical and not
with scientific knowledge. If science is interpretation and history is
interpretation too, another alleged distinguishing characteristic disappears. This view of historical knowledge marks a break with Collingwood's earlier theories: historical knowledge is no longer a mere assertion of facts, but an interpretation of them. Here the Copernican turn
in Collingwood's system provides the background for the attempt to
bring about a *rapprochement* between science and history.

The general line of this argument for the abolition of the clear-cut
distinction between history and science is one which shows the affinity
between science and history in two ways. From the point of view of
the relation to the individual there is an historical element in science.
From the point of view of predication and interpretation there is a
scientific element in history. Thus this is a mutual *rapprochement* based
mainly on methodological and epistemological considerations.

c) Hitherto, Collingwood's conception of the individual had been in a
way a common-sense one: it connoted factual, concrete, unique in its
traits, and thus irreducible to rules and not definable in their terms.
The antithetic term to individuality in this sense was generality. Yet
the view of history as essentially the knowledge of the individual, was
rejected in *Speculum Mentis*. Philosophy attains to the concrete not as
something antithetical to the general, but by virtue of its involving
within itself the general. From this synthesis between the individual
and the general the *universal* is established, which is the *concrete general*.
Mind as conceived by and through philosophy is individual but all-embracing and hence universal. Generality connotes – according to this distinction – a trait outside the individual and separated from it through
abstraction, whereas universality includes the individual. Philosophy as
an understanding of the world in its totality, philosophy as an understanding of the mind in all its manifestations, attains the level of universality. All this is clearly in the line of Hegel's distinctions.

With the change which took place in Collingwood's conception of
history and its relation to philosophy, there arose again the problem of
the relation between individuality and generality. Collingwood could
not retain his former conception of individuality in the realm of history,
since this conception was in its essence linked with the assumption of

the difference between philosophy and history on the one hand, and history and science on the other. A philosophical history could not use individual concepts if individuality connotes pure immediacy. Yet the question still remained open as to the sense in which history can be considered to be *universal*. The universality of philosophy was tied up with the notion of a *Weltgeist* which embraces and includes totality. Universality was actually realized in totality. Can this meaning of universality be applied to history?

Let us quote Collingwood himself:

The vague phrase that history is knowledge of the individual claims for it a field at once too wide and too narrow: too wide, because the individuality of perceived objects and natural facts and immediate experiences falls outside its sphere...; too narrow, because it would exclude universality, and it is just the universality, of an event or character that makes it a proper and possible object of historical study, if by universality we mean something that oversteps the limits of merely local and temporal existence and possesses a significance valid for all men at all times.[69]

Individuality is here understood not as immediate and purely factual, occurring once and confined to the limits of its occurrence. There is a meaning attached to individuality which is distinct from the former one. The new conception of history elevates facts to the mediated realm of thought. This may be considered as the negative definition of universality: that which is not immediate. The positive description of universality stresses that which is meaningful beyond the circumstances of its actual-temporal occurrence; universality in this sense is the very presupposition of historical knowledge. Universality is thus not opposite to concreteness, universality connoting here meaningfulness.

Prima facie, this meaning of universality, which is characteristic of the realm of history, is different from the meaning of universality *qua* totality as encountered in philosophy. Yet there is an important common feature which, we may justifiably assume, directed Collingwood in his search for the new meaning of universality though he has not as yet analysed it. In a way the meeting between the historical agent's thought and the re-enacting thought of the historian takes place in the realm of meaning. It is the meaning which is re-thought and not the act of thinking. In idealistic terms we might say that the meeting takes place in the domain of mind, i.e. in the domain of totality envisaged through philosophy. There is no identity between universality in philosophy and universality in history, as there is no identity between the two forms of cognition in general. History presupposes the totality envisaged in

[69] *The Idea of History*, p. 303.

philosophy. Totality is the domain where the concept of meaningfulness is possible altogether. This is by no means a summary of Collingwood's own line of argument, but it seems that this could serve as a critical elaboration of his idea.

From the point of view of the nature of the relationship between history and science we have to emphasize that, as a result of the new conception of individuality, the main trait which differentiates science and history disappears. The first step towards the abolition of the clear-cut differences between the two kinds of knowledge was made through the analysis which showed that the intention of science, too, is to conceive individuals. Thus the reference to individuals cannot be a distinctive trait of history alone. The second step was made through the analysis which showed that history, too, does not refer to individuals in the factual sense of the word. In the first place Collingwood demonstrated that science is like history; in the second place he demonstrated that history is like science.

d) The historicist impact on Collingwood's thought brought about a re-formulation of the problem of the relation between science and history. In Collingwood's historicism we have, in the first place, to emphasize the notion that the historical process is a process of perpetual change, thereby attacking all that could be considered as permanent. The idea of perpetual change is formulated by Collingwood as the idea of function as against structure. In a machine – he says – and therefore in nature if nature is mechanical, structure and function are distinct, and function presupposes structure. In the world of human affairs as known to the historian, there is no such distinction and *a fortiori* no such priority. Structure is resolvable into function. There is no harm in historians talking about the structure of feudal society or of capitalist industry or of the Greek city-state, but the reason why there is no harm in it is because they know that these so-called structures are really complexes of function, kinds of ways in which human beings behave.[70] The difference between the mechanistic ("old") science and history understood from the historicist point of view lies in the relation of the two kinds of knowledge to the concepts of structure and function respectively. Science, according to Collingwood, is characterized by two traits: (1) the very use of the notion of structure and (2) the priority of structure as against activity or function. History, on the other hand, does not presuppose the notion of structure at all, because of its Hera-

[70] See *The Idea of Nature*, pp. 16–17.

clitean nature. The old distinction, based on the extension of concepts (general *versus* individual), is replaced by a new distinction based upon the antithesis between the permanent and the change of less process, or upon the distinction between a static structure as against a total dynamics. The employment of structural concepts in the human realm – concepts like "feudal society" etc. – is actually an abbreviation which points to ways of behaviour or to what Max Weber used to call *the chance* that this or that behaviour will eventually take place. It should be mentioned that Collingwood did not consider the relation between history and the social sciences and did not raise the question of whether within the realm of human affairs there is still justification for taking advantage of structural concepts; nor did he affirm that the social sciences actually employ such concepts. Even if structures as such do not exist in the human realm, they are conceptual perspectives introduced in order to conceive of, and understand, a fragment of human existence. The impact of social sciences on philosophy of history comes to the fore in a later period of modern English philosophy of history, and will be shown in a later chapter of this book.[71]

In any case, we may say that the impact of historicism on Collingwood's thought moves the problem of science *versus* history from the assumption of the ultimate essence of reality as one composed of individuals to be conceived, to the assumption of different *categories* (structures *versus* functions) employed by the two branches of knowledge respectively.

e) The notion of the ontological and epistemological status of the factual *versus* the hypothetical was already expounded in *Speculum Mentis*. Since, according to the conception of *Speculum Mentis*, history deals with the factual while science creates the hypothetical through its chain of suppositions, history has itself a priority over science, although only *for us;* that is to say that in the dialectical development of the system it appears as a successive form of Mind, succeeding science. In the reformulation of the problem in *The Idea of Nature*, Collingwood retains the same idea, yet he expounds it in a somewhat strange form: "An event in the world of nature becomes important for the natural scientist only on condition that it is observed. ... The observer must have recorded his observation in such a way that knowledge of what he has observed is public property. ... Every scientist who says that Newton

---

[71] See the present author's "On Lévi-Strauss' Concept of Structure", *The Review of Metaphysics*, Vol. XXV, No. 3, March 1972, pp. 489–526.

observed the effect of a prism on sunlight . . . is talking history. . . . A scientific theory not only rests on certain historical facts . . . it is itself an historical fact."[72] It is evident that Collingwood here confused the nature of scientific knowledge with the ways in which communication of the knowledge is transmitted from man to man or from generation to generation. Scientific knowledge does not rest on the fact that Newton observed a fact; it rests on the observed fact itself. If scientific knowledge relies on the report made by Newton, it does so on two grounds, for technical-didactic and for epistemological reasons. Technically, not everybody is capable of carrying out the observation of the fact which is the evidence of the theory; one is therefore forced to rely on an authority who serves as the mediator between oneself and the observed scientifically significant fact. In terms of epistemological considerations, we must take cognizance here of a fundamental assumption, namely that everybody *can* make the same observation since the observed facts are public and open to everybody. Therefore it is unnecessary that everybody should actually carry out the observation and it is sufficient that Newton, for instance, made this observation. The observation is repeatable because it does not reveal something mysterious and does not presuppose super-human capacities in order to observe it. Therefore we may refrain from carrying it out ourselves, and are entitled to rely on somebody else, subject to the necessary limitations of reliance on authorities.

Yet we are obliged to raise a question: What is it that drove Collingwood to formulate this strange view as to the historical nature of natural science? Apparently there are two main reasons for the formulation of his idea: in the first place Collingwood's guiding light in this field was historicism, although historicism in a different sense from that pointed out before where historicism connoted a view of the universal as perpetually changing. Historicism here means the conception that everything is historical, that is to say that the historical perspective of understanding reality is the supreme one, being all-embracing. To prove this, one comes to see science (i.e. a branch of knowledge which in terms of its subject-matter and its method alike is considered to be different from history and even competing with it), as an historical discipline. The confusion between *science* and *communication of scientific results* is in the last resort an outcome of the conversion to historicism.

Yet there might be another reason as well. Collingwood in his late system assumed as the main feature of history the identity between

[72] *Ibid.*, pp. 176–177.

the knower and the known object, an identity realized in the realm of
the knower. The knower amounts to the mind of the real historian,
acting here and now, and understanding here and now the thoughts of
the historical agent. The knower is not a kind of "consciousness in
general," in terms of a relevant system of categories and of concepts.
He is an actual human being. This feature of history, namely its essential connection with an actually living knower, may be considered the
characteristic of history because it involves a knowledge of data in the
present and that the present is the dimension of reality and of man
living in reality. Collingwood, however, extends the idea of the personal
nature of historical knowledge to the nature of scientific knowledge:
he considers even in the domain of science the *knowing scientist and not
the known fact*. The impersonal nature of science, its methodological
essence in which methods replace genius (if we may paraphrase here
a saying of Bacon) is reduced to a personal knowledge. But actually
this leads Collingwood to a confusion of *science* with the *history of science*.
The concern with a scientific theory for its own sake is an object of the
history of science, while the nature of science is to deal with phenomena
explained by a scientific theory. But the history of science is an historical discipline, and therefore the logic of the re-enactment of thought
holds good for this discipline as for any other historical discipline. To
reduce science to history of science, unless it is a *lapsus linguae*, is an
indication of historicism pushed to its extreme, and carried *ad absurdum*.

f) Lastly the impact of history in terms of the emergence of the idea
of evolution has to be mentioned. "The victory of evolution in scientific
circles meant that the positivistic reduction of history to nature was
qualified by a partial reduction of nature to history."[73] If history is
understood as a process of changes, then nature understood as a process
of evolution is a realm understood in a historical fashion. According to
the evolutionist doctrine history overrides nature: not only is the scientific theory proper an historical occurrence, but nature itself is historical in its essence. This triumph of the historical perspective is
supposed to abolish the independence of the competing scientific perspective.

We may sum up this discussion by pointing to three ways of considering the relation between history and science in Collingwood:

(1) There is the *methodological way*: the relation between the two
branches of knowledge in terms of their connection with general and

---

[73] *The Idea of History*, p. 129. Compare the last chapter of *The Idea of Nature*.

individual concepts, in terms of their employment of structural and functional concepts, and lastly in terms of their epistemological priority over each other.

(2) There is the *material-conceptual way*: this consideration shows mainly the impact of history on the material concept of modern natural science in terms of the concept of evolution.

(3) There is the *evaluative way*: this consideration shows the relation between history and science in terms of their position in the universe of mind or man. In almost all the phases of his system, Collingwood places history above science: either because of its closeness to reality, or because of its status within the identity of subject and object, or because of its value in solving the problems which humanity faces in our age.

5. *History and politics*

a) In the late stage of his philosophical development Collingwood's thought was expressed in the dictum that "the so-called science of human nature or of the human mind resolves itself into history."[74] From this point of view the relationship between politics and history became of necessity a problem for Collingwood when he turned his thoughts to the nature of politics and the political situation of Europe in the twentieth century.

In his political treatise, *The New Leviathan*, one finds scattered remarks about history in general and about the historical nature of politics in particular, though Collingwood failed in this book to examine closely the assumptions that underlie his view of history as related to politics.

The idea that history is a history of thought, which may be considered Collingwood's main idea in this final stage of his thinking, appears also in the context of his political analysis. This idea can be formulated in its new context as follows: there is no way of dealing with human nature except by considering mind. The main problems of politics – discussion, ways of life and civilisation, war and peace, etc. are all problems of mind. "Civilisation is a thing of mind."[75] "War is a state of mind."[76] Since the political situation and political problems are states and problems of mind, our approach to them must be similar to

[74] *The Idea of History*, p. 220.
[75] *The New Leviathan*, p. 280.
[76] *Ibid.*, p. 229.

the approach to mind and its nature: "The answer to any question in any science of mind is provided by reflection."[77] The main characteristic feature of mind was considered (e.g. in *The Idea of History*) to be reflection, reflection being thought about thought. Reflection in this sense is the underlying capacity of historical thought, *qua* re-enactment of thought. Now, Collingwood in his analysis of politics advanced the same view of mind as in his analysis of history.

Yet the fact that the context is political coloured to some measure his discussion of the nature of mind. In politics one deals with problems to be solved, problems which in the classical view are regarded as *practical*. The content of practical problems led Collingwood to an extreme statement: "Social consciousness, like all forms of consciousness, is primarily a practical consciousness, not a "making up your mind *that*" but "a making up your mind *to*."[78] This is an extreme statement because it may lead us to question Collingwood's own description of historical consciousness. "In order to know anything I must not only be conscious, I must reflect on that consciousness. This reflection on simple consciousness I call second order consciousness...."[79] The question must be posed whether the practical essence of consciousness is to be taken as characteristic of the first-order consciousness, or else whether it has to be extended to include the second-order consciousness as well. The fact that Collingwood considered consciousness to be practical may account for the fact that he considered historical reflection to be concerned with thought as planning, that is to say with thought as practical. But historical consciousness proper, being in its nature a consciousness about thought and about consciousness in the first-order, cannot be understood as practical consciousness. This being so, we have to distinguish between the realm of practice which is the realm of historical data, and the realm of theory and reflection which is the realm of historical consciousness proper. This distinction would, however, run counter to Collingwood's main concern to establish the identity of historical object and historical subject, since it would place the object in the realm of practice and the subject in the realm of theory. The identity would not be established because of the difference in the character of the respective realms.

From the point of view of Collingwood's theory of mind, one further problem comes to the fore precisely when things are dealt with in the

[77] *Ibid.*, p. 6.
[78] *Ibid.*, p. 139.
[79] *Ibid.*, p. 20.

political context, namely the problem of the relationship between mind and facts in time. Civilisation, it has been said before, is a state of mind. But "civilisation is not civilisation but barbarity unless it insists that you shall treat every member of your community as civilly as possible; it is not a civilisation but Utopia unless it distinguishes occasions on which you simply must be civil, from others on which you may be. . . . uncivil."[80] If we analyse this view closely, we notice that civilisation is a state of mind as well as behaviour; on the other hand, in terms of the historical development of the process in time it is an intermediate status: barbarism and Utopia connote both states of mind and historical positions, as the starting point of history and its *eschaton* respectively. The question which the political context imposed on Collingwood was of necessity the relationship between mind and time. The time-factor which he considered as irrelevant for history, as analysed before, comes back again through the rear door, once the political problems are integrated in the whole theory.

b) Collingwood would prefer, as a matter of principle, to retain the view of time as irrelevant precisely because he talks about mind and the connection between human situation and mind. "Unlike progress . . . development does not imply time."[81] Development is a logical category and as such does not refer to the occurrence in time. But the human situation dealt with in politics is not a logical situation. The colouring of the philosophy of mind by the consideration of the nature and the status of politics leads Collingwood now to put forward the category of becoming: "Every case of mental 'being,' so-called, turns out on examination to be a case of mental 'becoming.' To describe a community as being in a state of civility... is a way of saying that it is undergoing a process of civilization...."[82] The process in time turns out to be essential for the mental reality – this is a conclusion to be drawn from Collingwood's statement. This time-factor that has been neglected in the realm of history comes back into history *via* the realm of politics. It is clear however, that the time-factor cannot be decisive in the mental reality in its political expression, since it is not decisive in its historical expression in general, because history is the locus of politics. To regard time as essential for politics without conceding the value due to it in history, is to give it the status of a *deus ex machina*. Precisely because

[80] *Ibid.*, p. 292.
[81] *Ibid.*, p. 64.
[82] *Ibid.*, p. 285.

the time-factor is involved in politics, the surmise advanced earlier as
to the twofold meaning of the status of civilisation is explicitly con-
firmed by Collingwood, namely that civilisation is both a state of mind
and a situation in time and in the historical process. Actually, we are
involved in "a change from condition of relative *barbarity* to one of
relative *civility*."[83] The stress put on the *relative* aspect is correlative
to the stress on the historical *qua* changing and open to the changing
nature of the situation. Furthermore: historical things are said to come
into existence gradually,[84] that is to say in and through a process in
time. It is the time-factor which makes the difference between one
stage of barbarity and another.[85] In all these observations Collingwood
takes for granted the commonsense view of history as a process in time
and implicitly – – abandons his own systematic position. It is difficult
to say whether the new estimation of time points to a change in Collingwood's own fundamental position or whether it is the impact of the
subject matter that compelled him to restore the same factor which he
disposed of when he dealt with history systematically.

c) In terms of the explicit view of history which we now find restated
in *The New Leviathan*, it is apposite to point out an additional aspect.

History is the science of the individual; the individual is the unique; the unique
is the only one of its kind, the possible which is also necessary. The more a man
accustoms himself to thinking historically, the more he will accustom himself to
thinking what course of action it is his duty to do, as distinct from asking what
is expedient for him to do and what it is right for him to do... "because it was
his duty."[86]

(1) Collingwood starts here with the assumption that history deals
with individuals. But he carries this assumption to its extreme by
introducing two modal concepts: possibility and necessity. Each occasion, being individual, is unique. Since it is unique, there is no other
occasion that shares the same essence with it. As with Leibniz, the
notion of essence is implied here in the term "possibility." But at this
point Collingwood produces a kind of ontological or even supra-onto-
logical argument from possibility to necessity. He says that the event
is possible, and since there is a possibility of each occasion being different from the possibility of any other occasion – what is possible is also
necessary. He does not even say that what is possible is *real* but con-

[83] *Ibid.*, p. 289.
[84] Cf. *ibid.*, p. 376.
[85] Cf. *ibid.*, p. 380.
[86] *Ibid.*, p. 221.

siders the transition from possibility to *necessity* as legitimate. This paradoxical statement is tantamount to saying that because history is concerned with individuals it is *eo ipso* concerned with necessities. When modern philosophy – and in this it resembles classical philosophy – maintains that history is the domain of the individual, it takes up this position from the viewpoint of a theory which considers the individual as contradicting the necessary. By contrast, Collingwood stresses the identity of the individual and the necessary.

(2) History, and Collingwood says this clearly, deals with deeds and their results. But history starts with results and by way of regression or re-enactment enters upon the deed. History thus starts with the existent and from it approaches the possible. Yet the possible is, in Collingwood's view, the necessary, because "To think historically is to explore a world consisting of things other than myself, each of them an individual or unique agent, in an individual or unique action ... which he has to do because, charactered and circumstanced as he is, he can do no other."[87] Necessity in this sense is tantamount to the full determination by the character of the agent on the one hand, and of the circumstances he is involved in, on the other. It is, to say the least, not clear how Collingwood could arrive at this deterministic individualism (or else, how he could adopt a point of view which sees Spinoza transplanted to the domain of Leibniz) and at the same time retain the fundamental view of history as rooted in mind.

(3) Yet the necessity in the deterministic sense is given a moral turn. To do what character and circumstance impose on the agent is to perform a duty. "A man's duty on a given occasion is the act which for him is both possible and necessary: the act which at that moment character and circumstance combine to make it inevitable, if he has a free will, that he should freely will to do."[88] We notice that the terms "possibility" and "necessity" are found in a context dealing with the exploration of the concept of duty, just as they were found earlier in the context of the discussion of the historical individual. But in the moral context Collingwood adds the decisive factor: it is the free will which has to acknowledge and to accept the determination of the inner and external situation. The moral view here is one of *"my station and its duties."* The new feature in Collingwood's theory of history is the import of the moralistic aspect in that theory. But precisely because of this combination, the whole view of acknowledging the situation

[87] *Ibid.*, p. 128.
[88] *Ibid.*, p. 124.

and turning its determination into an acceptance of a duty sounds rather like *amor fati*.

(4) Again we may consider this view in the light of Collingwood's historicism. One can consider the relationship existing between the historical view and the concept of duty as abolishing historicism because of the very fact that the moral concept of duty is introduced into the realm of historical analysis. The moral evaluation becomes part of the historical outlook. But actually the introduction of the concept of duty does not mitigate historicism; it even underlines it. Because the act of duty is eventually identical with the act of morally affirming the given situation, there is no sense of transcending the situation and acting in spite of it, as if in accord with a moral trans-situational imperative. Because the concept of the situation is central and is emphasized by employing ontological categories (possibility and necessity), Collingwood's historicism reasserts itself in spite of the fact that he has to abandon it when dealing with politically historical phenomena like civilisation *versus* barbarism where his sympathy is clearly with civilisation.

This last point brings us to a consideration of what may be called Collingwood's historiosophy as against his theory of history.

d) The shift from an individualistic determinism to a denial of historical evaluation comes to the fore in Collingwood's remarks about one specific material historical concept, i.e. revolution. Collingwood considers revolution to be a concept rooted in, or at least implying, an evaluation, or as he puts it – self-identification. "You must identify yourself, as you read, with the character who succeeds after temporary success. You must think of historical characters as 'heroes' and 'villains.' . . . But if you write or read history to get at truth you must not do it."[89] It is by no means evident why Collingwood considered the concept of revolution to be a value-concept and as such alien to the historical approach proper. Revolution may connote a fundamental change in a society when, for example, one legal system is replaced by another legal system, say by use of force, without however implying that when we employ such a concept we identify ourselves positively as "heroes" or negatively as "villains" with the event of the revolution or with its protagonists. It seems as if Collingwood at this point wanted to stress the necessary occurrence of a revolution and hence proceed

[89] *Ibid.*, p. 201.

to stress its necessary character by rejecting the appropriateness of a moral evaluation.

Furthermore: Collingwood attacked the very legitimacy of the concept of revolution. The way he rejects the legitimacy of that concept reveals the meaning of the individuality and uniqueness of an historical event. "To stop being surprised when the course of history waggles, and to think of it as waggling all the time." "Historians today know that all history consists of changes, and that all these changes involve 'reversals of fortune.' But the historical idea of a revolution implies that normally the course of history flows, as if by the Newtonian First Law of Motion, uniformly in a straight line; then it waggles, and you are surprised."[90] Is it possible to find in Collingwood's own thought a basis for this observation as to the material rhythm of the historical process in terms of principles?

This observation about the waggly character of the historical process is but a material interpretation or translation of the uniqueness of the historical events. What is considered to be unique in terms of content turns out to be an atomistic event. Uniformity is a denial of uniqueness – this could be a possible rendering of the position Collingwood takes as to the nature of the historical process.

Now, it can be questioned whether Collingwood was right on this point both in terms of the adequacy of his observation and in terms of the principle he himself maintains. The uniqueness of the event does not abolish the fact that there are different historical events in terms of the pace of the process, i.e. in terms of the rapid change they introduce or are claimed to introduce. The concept of revolution may be retained as a concept applicable to the historical process, e.g. if we distinguish between changing events within the given framework of a society and events which attack the very framework of the society. A revolution would then be an event which tries to replace the existing framework, and from this point of view the American Revolution or the French Revolution etc. are not just *flatus vocis* as Collingwood is inclined to think, but descriptions of real changes occurring in a given society and within a "pregnant" period of time.

The problem in terms of principles which emerges here concerns the shift from a formal concept of uniqueness to a material concept of the historical rhythm. The formal description of historical events as being unique is by no means a basis for a material interpretation of the meaning of historical events. The test for the validity of the formal

[90] *Ibid.*, pp. 200, 201.

concepts lies in material historical events and not *vice versa*. A disregard for the limits of the formal description of historical events leads to a schematic view of history and to a kind of historical *a-priorism*. It has already been shown that Collingwood was inclined to this kind of *a-priorism* mainly because of his attempt to ground history in mind. But for precisely this reason the analysis of his view of revolution exhibits the limits and the dangers of a formalistic construction of history.

Collingwood was misled by his determinism in his discussion of the concept of revolution. This can be seen from the fact that he considers the concept of revolution to be analogous to the concept of chance. "If a physicist said 'That happened by chance,' he would be saying 'I don't know why it happened and it surprised me.' Similarly if an historian said 'That was revolution'."[91] The analogy drawn between the concept of revolution and that of chance is intended to indicate that the concept of revolution is a kind of *asylum ignorantiae*. Hence it is to be rejected once it is understood that whatever happens in history had to happen for the reason that what is possible is necessary. Here again all this could be valid if one assumed that the revolution breaks the causal chain of the historical process. The fact that we maintain the view that whatever happened had to happen does not preclude that the event which happened was a revolutionary event. Again the formal consideration of the historical process, granted its validity, does not preclude *a priori* any specific view as to the material character of events under discussion.

e) The preceding analysis allows us to state as a matter of fundamental consideration that in connection with the problem of politics and more specifically in connection with the crisis of the "European mind," Collingwood's view of history shifts from a consideration stated in terms of historical cognition to one stated in terms of historical process.

In Collingwood's analysis of history as history of thought, and of historical knowledge as re-enactment, the understanding that history is essentially intelligible was already implied. Thought as the subject-matter of history provides for its intelligibility, while the identity of the historical subject with his object is an additional factor in guaranteeing that intelligibility. In the context of the political analysis a new feature in Collingwood's view of history is brought into relief: history is not only intelligible because it is open to re-enactment; it is reason-

[91] *Ibid.*, p. 201.

able in itself. As Collingwood puts it, arguing in a Hegelian way, the reasonable nature of history presents itself to those who take part in the spectacle of history intelligently.[92] We have to consider now the concrete manifestations of reason in history.

The main notion which expresses the rational essence of the historical or at least of the political process is the notion of dialectic: "political life is essentially dialectical."[93] Collingwood introduces the notion of dialectic in what he considers to be the Platonic view of dialectic, though in his former writings he suggested some different interpretations of the notion of dialectic in Plato.[94] Yet now in the political context he says: "Dialectic ... is Plato's name for a peaceful, friendly discussion in which the disputants aim at agreement, as opposed to a discussion embittered or rendered warlike by their aiming at victory."[95] But actually Collingwood enlarges or enhances the notion of dialectic. Dialectic does not connote for him only a method of discussion. The method of discussion is concerned with the objective position of the problem and with the pros and cons in the discussion. "The essence of dialectical discussion is to discuss in the hope of finding that both parties to the discussion are right."[96] The friendly manner of the discussion is related to a view of the validity of the views involved in the discussion. This manner is only an expression of the fact that there is no point in a victory because there is no side which can, on its merits, be victorious. Furthermore: "In a dialectical discussion you aim at showing that your view is one with which your opponent really agrees, even if at one time he denied it; or conversely that it was yourself and your opponent who began by denying a view with which you really agree."[97] In this description of the dialectical situation one can clearly see that in such a situation a broad view is taken in spite of the fact that the opponents involved are not aware of it. There is a difference between the – objectively – right view which occupies a position by itself and the views held by the opponents. In a dialectical situation the right view comprises in itself the two opposite views. This breadth of view is an expression of the reason involved in dialectic. Reason is understood here as impersonal, above the partial and personal views of the opponents. The fact that dialectic is related to a friendly method

---

[92] *Ibid.*, p. 207.
[93] *Ibid.*, p. 208.
[94] Compare *Speculum Mentis*, p. 77; *An Essay on Philosophical Method*, pp. 100ff.; *An Essay on Metaphysics*, pp. 156ff.
[95] *The New Leviathan*, p. 277.
[96] *Ibid.*, pp. 181–182.
[97] *Ibid.*, p. 181.

of discussion is but an expression of its relation and its grounding in reason, reason being the total view.

In effect, the notion of dialectic as the main notion of politics has replaced the concept of compromise as it is usually understood in politics. A compromise is a *de facto* agreement; the opponents agree to find a minimum common to both of them, because the fact is that there are different views of interests. Practical politics is impossible unless there is a *post-factum* minimum common ground between the factors involved in political life. This is not Collingwood's view: dialectics overcomes the partiality of one's one-sided position, not in order to meet the opponent's point, but in order to replace any one-sided position with what is by reason the true view because it is a broad view.

Precisely at this point the concept of politics appears to be related to the concept of history. History is essentially dialectical and if it becomes for a while non-dialectical it regresses to a barbaric stage of its process. "*Being civilized* means *living, so far as possible, dialectically*, that is, in constant endeavour to convert every occasion of non-agreement into an occasion of agreement."[98] Once there is no constant effort of this sort, the opponents struggle for victory and not for agreement. In this case the relation between the opposing principles becomes *eristical* instead of being dialectical.

What must be pointed out in this view is that Collingwood transferred philosophical methods to the realm of politics and history. In a way Collingwood is not aware of the fact that he, like Marx, looks at politics as at a realization of philosophy. The two possibilities of politics either agreement or war, are but expressions of two possible philosophical views, dialectical and eristical. Collingwood now considers history and politics to be an expression of a philosophical rhythm of dialectic and eristic.

Yet history is rational not only by virtue of being an expression of philosophical positions, but mainly because it provides the victory of the true philosophical position, that of dialectic. In the first place, Collingwood sees the replacement of the dialectical process with the eristical process not only as dangerous for civilization but also as illusory. In the real historical process as it presents itself to a rational onlooker, the dialectical rhythm is inherent. "Throughout European history from at least the times of ancient Greece, democracy and aristocracy ... have gone hand in hand as the positive and negative elements of a dialectical development, democracy always promoting

[98] *Ibid.*, p. 326.

the inclusion of competent recruits from the ruled class into the ruling class, aristocracy always checking that process when the candidates were thought unsuitable."[99] The disregard for the essentially dialectical nature of the process creates an eristic process and along with it eristic politics. But this change from dialectic to eristic is imaginary; at the very least, by its nature it creates or gives rise to a reaction. "... (it) means the replacement of a dialectical process in which the two cooperate by a continuation of the imaginary eristic; the thing supposed to be vanquished (it is not really vanquished) engages in a war of revenge and tries, or rather its partisans try, to inflict a crushing blow on the thing falsely supposed to be victorious."[100] It seems that we are entitled to say that not only is there a revenge on the part of the opposite side which was defeated, but there is a revenge on the part of the dialectical principle itself. The reaction created by the defeat establishes not only the defeated opponent, but vindicates the dialectical principle as such. Collingwood acknowledges the barbarian breakdown in history, but ultimately the rational nature of history provides for an optimistic outlook: "the defeat of barbarism, I say, is always certain in the long run."[101] He adds however at this point that he does not know the reason for the fact that barbarians have always been beaten in the end. Yet it seems as if this is an understatement, because reason in history is, in the last analysis, the reason for the defeat of barbarism. Civilization and not barbarism is the adequate manifestation of the nature of reason and hence in the long run civilization defeats the anti-rational barbarism.

We may now sum up this discussion and at the same time the whole critical exposition of Collingwood's theory of history: Collingwood defined the subject-matter of history as thought. This definition enables him to advance a fragment of philosophy of history prompted by his main view on the one hand, and by the Nazi experience on the other. He expanded his former formal view of history by a view which replaces thought with reason and provides a basis for optimism in an age of crisis. But once Collingwood went over to a historiosophical speculation, he had to make room for the time-factor and to consider history not only as a way of knowing human nature but also as a process. This is a paradoxical turn: the rational nature of history enabled Collingwood to acknowledge the position of time, though time itself is given

99 *Ibid.*, p. 206.
100 *Ibid.*, p. 207.
101 *Ibid.*, p. 348.

and irrational. The crisis in civilization being a living reality, and the realm of politics being a "becoming," reminded Collingwood of what he had in a way forgotten in the system of historical knowledge which he established.[102]

[102] Consult Lionel Rubinoff, *Collingwood and the Reform of Metaphysics, A Study in the Philosophy of Mind*, Toronto, 1970.

CHAPTER II

THE PREJUDICE OF INEVITABILITY:
ISAIAH BERLIN

I.

If metaphysics is understood as the comprehensive study of all the fields of human activities, then R. G. Collingwood was – until now – the last metaphysician to occupy the chair of Metaphysics in modern English philosophical life. The fact that he has been succeeded in the chair of Metaphysics by Gilbert Ryle has its parallel, more dramatic in terms of political beliefs but less dramatic in the very meaning of the subject-matter, in M. Oakeshott's succeeding Harold Laski in the chair of Political Science.

The development of modern English philosophy in its analytic trend disregarded to a large extent the problem of history as process and, significantly, shifted to the question of historical explanation. The concern with history in terms of its position within the synoptic philosophical system disappeared along with the change of the philosophical climate of opinion.

In the new generation engaged in philosophical analysis of history, we encounter more an analysis of concrete problems, problems having an empirical meaning within one's empirical-historical experience. We do not encounter an analysis of the position of history from the point of view of the development of Spirit in the Hegelian sense, which was in the last resort, as we have seeen, the point of departure for Collingwood and remained his favourite theme in all the changes his thought underwent. One of the concrete historical problems is that of historical prediction and inevitability. From the point of view of this shift towards a detailed and yet fundamental aspect of history and historical experience we are about to deal with Sir Isaiah Berlin's contribution to philosophy of history.

Yet, before proceeding to this task let us insert an observation of a general character.

2.

In present-day philosophy, one finds a tendency to disregard, or at least to re-interpret distinctions, common in some schools of thought, which not too long ago were considered hard and fast. Thus, for example, it is doubtful whether the distinction between speculation and experience is as clear-cut as it once was, at least so far as seventeenth and eighteenth century thinkers were concerned. Existentialist philosophy, e.g., while adhering to experience and seeking to determine its structures, at the same time probes into speculative-ontological questions. Speculation takes it upon itself to comply with the demands of rational deliberation imposed by reason itself and binding upon all who undertake to offer a rational account of theoretical problems and judgments. The rise of the natural sciences and the scientific optimism that followed in their wake strengthened the theoretical-rational position and sponsored the formulation of purportedly synoptic views of reality, and encouraged the formulation of others as more and more vistas are opened for man's surveyal. Thus whereas not long ago synoptic world-pictures were deemed speculative or metaphysical, today they are often called scientific. This is the reason for the emergence of a philosophical criticism of scientific conprehensiveness. *Pari passu* with this criticism goes that of the demand for an unambiguous world-outlook, in so far as a comprehensive view, be it scientific or of another nature, pretends to form such a view.

Turning to other intellectual spheres one finds that they too feature a blurring of school-distinctions or a novel interpretation of their meaning. Thus in literary criticism the traditional categories are no longer adequate in view of the profusion of literary creations which make a point of breaking all the "rules." Hence there is obviously a need for new criteria of classification and evaluation which might clear theory of its stock of wooden distinctions and permit a fresh appraisal of the phenomena at hand. The same is true of political theory which is confronted by a multifarious variety of political phenomena that cannot be exhaustively defined in terms of the types of regime discerned by classical and even nineteenth century political thought.

That English philosophy has taken the lead in the trend towards blunting the edge of scholastic distinctions is only understandable, considering its age-long tradition of fusing empiricism and science. It is also to be noted that it is to the natural sciences that British philosophy has always turned when seeking a scientific ground of truth. Was it not

Hume who demanded that philosophy adopt the method of natural sciences when dealing with matters of mind? And did he not conceive of a scientific philosophy as a strictly empirical one? Turning to the British philosophers concerned mainly with political problems, and especially to Hobbes, we find that they too have always mingled the methodical precision of the natural sciences with empirical observation of the manifold of concrete facts when dealing with problems of social and political life. Perhaps the most representative expression of this trend to have emerged in the last generation is the work of Bertrand Russell. Last generation – so far as the dominant ideas and range of influence are concerned, though Russell was still an active participant in the philosophical world early in the present generation. In present-day English philosophy there are signs, faint but still clear, of a divorce between the scientific and the empirical schools. One such indication is the growing prestige of "common sense" as a mode of cognition in its own right, independent of scientific method and, in its own sphere, not inferior to the scientific mode of cognition. Thus several thinkers have undertaken to analyse the logic of every-day language and to formulate what Gilbert Ryle thought to be an informal and unofficial logic. This coinage in itself testifies to the fact that the analytical philosophy constitutes a sort of reaction to the strict, formal logic of in the broadest and scientific modes of thought, science here being taken mathematical sense of the term.

Surprisingly enough, this shift has brought in its wake a new evaluation of traditional questions concerning, e.g. the relation between freedom and necessity, between man as an active agent and the automatic course of events, between personal responsibility and the anonymity of the impersonal historical process. In his most recent essays which we shall consider presently, Isaiah Berlin emerges as a thinker who, while influenced by the current directions of English philosophy, at the same time is working towards an independent approach which quite explicitly has recourse to traditional ideas.

3.

The climate of thought we have traced is clearly in the background of Berlin's censure of the idea of historical inevitability in his commemoration-lecture on Auguste Comte, the father of Posivitism and the author of the well-known scheme of the historical process-stages and who predicated the scientific stage as the forthcoming stage of history.

However, in his lecture Berlin[1] takes issue not with positivist thought but rather with Butterfield's Christian reading of history and with Toynbee's conception of an historical destiny, both views being tinged with the Romanticism of an attempted fusion of the basic tenets of diverse religions. Berlin does not go into the details of these systems. He is, rather, troubled by the popularity they have won among laymen and it is their growing influence that has led him to challenge their authority as a factor shaping the background of the average educated person. Berlin observes, and rightly so, that the words of the keepers of history's keys are lapped up hungrily by an entire generation; a generation faced with the bankruptcy of possible optimism, no longer satisfied with Comte's partly naïve, partly prophetic schema, and aware that the complexity of the modern world calls for a more intricate scheme whereby to comprehend it. Thus the very faith in comprehensive schemes is as strong as ever and the validity of its theoretical status seems to be unshaken. In view of the popularity of these theories, a thinker who seeks to re-instate the individual historical agent as capable of determining his own actions and even the course of events, must first of all expose the dogmatism of the unquestioned presupposition of all-encompassing historical patterns. True, neither Butterfield nor Toynbee avow their adherence to the natural sciences. On the contrary, their expressed aim is to establish the uniqueness of the historical process. Thus Butterfield conceives of history as a reflection of the evil principle innate in human nature, and Toynbee seeks a formulation of the immanent rhythm of historical cycles and of the rise and fall of civilizations. Nevertheless, these views have fallen prey to the charm of the natural sciences. To Berlin's mind, the very quest for patterns at once comprehensive and definite and the assumption of a stable, fixed element in the flux of events, are spurred by the great strides made by the natural sciences in the direction of classifying,schematizing and predicting natural occurrences. According to these views, the function of history as a science is to guide us in our search for immutable and invariable aspects of our existence. In this respect the historian and the natural scientist are impelled by one and the same motive. The urge to discover historical patterns parallel to the schemes of natural occurrences leads us to discard as unscientific whatever cannot be comprehended within such a pattern. Evaluation pertains to the realm of

[1] Isaiah Berlin, *Historical Inevitability*, London, 1954. Also, without special reference to the realm of history, Stuart Hampshire's *Thought and Action* (London,1959) has to be [placed in this context. Isaiah Berlin's essays are now included in his *Four Essays on Liberty*, London, Oxford, New York, 1969.

the subject, and is an expression of his personal standpoint, a stand-point which, so far as science is concerned, is redundant and fated to disappear once the objective pattern is discovered in its full compre-hensiveness and determination. In his book on Tolstoy, Berlin makes a point of Tolstoy's having seen clearly that if history is a science, it must be possible to discover and formulate a set of true laws of history. And such a set has not been, nor, according to Tolstoy, would ever be, discovered. Tolstoy even went so far as to assert that "if we allow that human life can be ruled by reason the possiblity of life (i.e. as a spontaneous activity involving consciousness of free will) is des-troyed."[2]

At this juncture, Berlin's treatment of the question of historical evaluations has to be supplemented by an observation. For one thing, an historical theory purporting to be scientific does not necessarily bar historical evaluation. There can be no doubt that the Marxist concep-tion of history, though purportedly scientific, does not overlook the question of historical evaluation nor does Butterfield's Christian view; nor does Toynbee's theory which is permeated by evaluations to such an extent that it is at times more evaluative than penetrating.[3]

Thus we may observe that to posit an historical pattern is not necessa-rily to forbid historical evaluation. However, it is true that evaluation takes on a different meaning in the Marxist and Christian views and it might be appropriate to devote a few words to this matter.

(1) As stated, the Marxist conception of history does allow room for evaluation which, however, is represented as the judgment of history upon itself. In other words, the historical process created historical forms, building new forms on the ruins of the old; historical evaluation signifies the historical victory of the new form over the old. Until the advent of a new historical form, historical evaluation of the present form is bound up with the anticipation, in the present, of the unborn form of the future. The partnership of the present with the future finds its concrete manifestation in the status and historical role of the prole-tariat. Hence, according to this theory, evaluation implies neither an estimate of the intrinsic worth of a specific event nor the passing of judgment upon an individual historical figure but rather constitutes an historical institution. Thus Berlin is quite right to observe that once

---

[2] *The Hedgehog and the Fox*, London, 1954, p. 14. It is not accidental that Berlin's article "History and Theory, The Concept of Scientific History" (*History and Theory*, Vol. I/1, 1960) opens with an Aristotelian description: "History is an account of what individual human beings have done and suffered."

[3] See the present author's *The Recurring Pattern, Studies in Anti-Judaism in Modern Thought*, London, 1963.

it is transformed into an historical institution, evaluation is compressed into an all-embracing historical mould with the result that the clear-cut distinction between an event and the individual evaluating it, is obviated. According to this view, the event itself carries with it an objective evaluation of its status, leaving, so to speak, the individual subject the sole function of reading the handwriting on its wall.

(2) The Christian interpretation, based upon the assumption that man is born evil, does not evaluate historical events as such, simply because it expects nothing of them. Since historical evil is but a reflection of man's evil nature, that is, of original sin, there is no sense in demanding anything of it or in conjecturing as to its meaning. The course of history is inevitable and that is all there is to it. If every historical evaluation presupposes, at least in principle, the possibility of alternative decisions or actions, and since the truth of the matter is that all decisions, evaluation included, are determined by our evil nature, what use is it to pass judgment on history? If judge we must, then it is on human nature that we must put the blame. Thus this view does not posit the existence of immutable historical patterns or fixed historical laws determining the individual, isolated event. It rather affirms the motive force of a single, permanent, immutable historical factor – namely human nature understood in terms of sin, since the historical process does not alter human nature but rather reveals it. The limited number of possibilities inherent in human nature affords no grounds for criticizing the direction history takes. And even were one to put the blame on human nature itself, his objection would not constitute a moral demand but would rather serve as the cornerstone for a doctrine of faith and Grace. For Grace alone can redeem the world from its Fall, from the state to which it has been reduced because of the evil principle ruling man. So long as man remains the citizen of the kingdom of Nature, his subjection to the evil principle is irremediable. According to this interpretation, taken in its radical form, history exists in order to be superseded by a trans-historical state independent of the historical process for its realization, that is, by the kingdom of Grace. Here, as in Marxism, we do find an historical evaluation of the present in the light of a future state. Here, too, the present state is fated to make way for another. Yet whereas Marxism does not preach a trans-historical state, the Christian view does. The historical present is to give way to the supra-historical state of Grace, the arrival of which is independent of history. In other words, admitting only one mode of existence, i.e. the historical, the Marxist conception anchors historical

evaluation in the historical process itself. The Christian conception, on the other hand, recognizes a trans-historical realm and therefore roots evaluation in an element transcending history. Thus whereas in the Marxist view evaluation becomes an historical institution, such as e.g. the class-struggle, in the Christian conception evaluation has been shorn of historical significance and import, and rather transfers the historical creature into a supra-historical kingdom of Grace. History belongs as it were to nature, whereas evaluation stems from Grace.

(3) In the Marxist conception of history one finds that the problem of historical evaluation is related to the question of historical forecast. In other words, this view asserts that the future itself is the moral criterion according to which historical events and agents up to the future are to be judged. The future is imbued with moral value not merely in its formal, temporal sense but also in its material sense, i.e. in the to-be-realized content with which it is pregnant. In assigning moral content to a dimension of time, Marxism sought to establish the possibility of an historical evaluation which would not be dependent on the arbitrary inclinations of the historian or of the historical agent. That is, it sought to establish an objective evaluation and to present the process evaluated as anchored from the outset in a realm which calls for evaluation, a realm which while factual, is at the same time morally significant by its very nature.

One may wonder why Berlin did not include the Marxist view in his discussion of the problem of historical evaluation and prediction. Apparently his interest in the problem of historical prediction is confined to those aspects which have bearing upon the question of personal responsibility. In other words, Berlin feels that a predictable and hence inevitable historical process eliminates the possibility of personal responsibility. A similar view is expressed by Karl R. Popper in his book *The Open Society and its Enemies*. By an Open Society, Popper understands a society whose future horizon is an open one and where individuals are confronted with personal decisions, that is, a future which may be shaped by the critical forces of man, but not foreseen, at least not in detail.[4] According to Popper, the enemies of the Open Society from Plato to Marx, closed off the horizon of the future by representing the future as a matter for prediction rather than for shaping. Popper, like Berlin, is nurtured by the tradition which combines empiricism and science, and like him he is concerned primarily

---

[4] Karl R. Popper, *The Open Society and its Enemies*, Vol. I, London, 1949, pp. 1, 152. See also the revealing dedication in his *Poverty of Historicism*, London, 1964.

with the moral problem of the individual's responsibility for his decisions and actions as well as, ultimately, for the historical process.

The question is whether Berlin has shown that in order to invalidate an historical theory it suffices to indicate that it bars personal responsibility, i.e. that it deprives the historical agent of his authority to decide upon, and thus to shape, the course of historical events. As we shall see later, Berlin is inclined to think that one can refute an historical theory by castigating it for denying the individual self-sponsored participation in the historical process. Yet it seems that if these theories are to be repudiated, one can do so only by way of a theoretical critique of their basic premises. And there are two theoretical questions which we may put to the proponents of inevitability amounting eventually to predictability:

(1) First of all, can the future, in the strict sense of the term, be made an object of forecast without contradiction? A predictable object is, in the last analysis, an object of contemplation, be it cognitive, philosophic or scientific. To say that the future is predictable is to say that it lends itself to contemplation, which in turn implies that, rather than constituting a dimension about to appear, the future has already appeared. Thus, paradoxically enough, to posit a predictable future makes it for all purposes a past, since past alone can be known or be an object of historical cognition in virtue of its traces in the present. Fix the future as a present, here already because predicated, and you cancel its futurity. Or else, if the fact of its remoteness in time is incompatible with its material presence, so much the worse for the facts. The assertion of a predictable future involves a contradiction between the fact of the future's temporal distance and the concept of its proximity in so far as its substance and content are concerned. Thus the proponents of predictability would be obliged to admit that temporal remoteness is not an essential feature of the nature of the future.

(2) Secondly, the possibility of forecast in the historical sphere is by no means established by referring to its possibility in the sphere of natural science. Yet there seem to be no other grounds for this assumption. Why is predictability of natural occurrences no warrant for the predictability of historical ones? For one thing, the "when" of the occurrence is irrelevant from the physical point of view but of key-importance from the point of view of history. For another, the historical event is not the mere fact that something has taken place. It is meaningful and its meaning can be grasped only by an participant who has encountered it, and not by a prophet who foresees it here and now.

The theory of historical predictability tends to blur this fundamental distinction between the very occurrence of an anticipated phenomenon, say an impending economic crisis, or a war about to break out on the one hand, and the meaning it will convey to tomorrow's citizens on the other. The meaning of today's future as the present of tomorrow's agents, as well as the future implications of today's future-realized, are clearly unpredictable. History as a *real* course of events involves not only the future of the present generation but the future of the future generation as well. Neither today's future, nor *a fortiori*, tomorrow's future is a simple continuation of the present.[5] Here time in its dimensions has to be taken seriously, and we point out again the aspect raised in the preceding analysis of Collingwood's theory.

In addition to these immanent difficulties connected with the theory of historical predictability, it is quite true that this view must come up against the problem of personal responsibility which cannot be solved on its premises. However, in dealing with this question we must bear in mind that we do not approach historical problems as disinterested observers, and that we must therefore be on our guard lest our moral "vested interests" sway our appraisal and analysis of the theoretical matter at hand. The crucial theoretical problem is whether historical responsibility is *possible;* to insist upon its desirability is not to establish its possibility. One way of establishing the possibility of historical responsibility would be to point out the fact that the future is not the past. In the automatic flow of the objective process towards the future, we are cast upon reefs of subjectivity where we find ourselves possessed of the power to shape, where we grasp the significance of events, where we experience history actively, where we no longer postpone deliberate experience, bequeathing to those who shall come after us, the future. As to the men of the future, they too shall no doubt postpone experience and live their present lives as if they were nothing but a passage to yet another future superseding the future which has already arrived, fully certain that a new future is about to arrive. Were it not for this game of postponements, there would be no ground for the distinction e.g. between the existing stage of socialism and the forthcoming stage of communism. Nor would there be any reason to repudiate, as the historical prophets do, criticism or evaluation of the present on the grounds that the future shall solve present problems of itself if we only carry out our present task to the best of our ability. Paradoxically enough,

---

[5] The problem of historical prediction has been analysed by the present author in *Between Past and Present, An Essay on History.*

assured of a predictable future man is at once flung into the empty space of the future and confined, so far as his actual life is concerned, to the present. In confining actual conduct to the present, the prophets of the future sanction all phases of this present, firmly convinced that the future shall redeem all its imperfections. Bolshevism is here a case in point.

4.

Perhaps the main point in Berlin's writings is the radical opposition between the ultimately impersonal nature of the comprehensive conceptions of history and the personal character of an interpretation of the historical process which allows for individual responsibility (see page 7 of *Historical Inevitability*). To Berlin's mind there is a difference between those who would weave everything into a single principle and those who pursue many ends often unrelated and even contradictory.[6] There can be no doubt that the proponent of a multiple-purpose theory is closer to human reality, a reality which permits no sweeping generalizations overshadowing the particulars, than is the proponent of a uni-purposed, single universal process; the process is not only abstracted from, but it is even alien to, the complexity of human existence. Of course it may be objected that a scientific theory necessarily implies generalizations and hence abstraction from the particulars, which are but variables inessential in a universal system of invariable factors. Thus Berlin has joined the ranks of those thinkers who through the ages have come to the defense of the concrete-particular by questioning the absolute authority of scientific generalizations and abstractions. He is quite an emphatic adherent of that historical conception which maintains the concrete and real multifariousness of human existence. In rebelling against the homogeneity of sweeping historical purposes, Berlin does not offer a full theoretical demonstration of his challenge. The decisive question which must be asked is whether it is possible to maintain an historical standpoint which ignores the essential features of human reality as it is, and forces it into comprehensive processes. To put it bluntly – what exactly are these generalizations driving at? Do they pretend to explain human existence in terms of its major direction and trends? Or do they rather purport to trace the complete and unitary plan of the process by casting aside the multiple by-ways as digressions rather than direc-

---

[6] See *The Hedgehog and the Fox*, p. 1; also "*History and Theory*", pp. 6–7. The political importance of this point will be analysed in the last section of this chapter.

tions in their own right? Before proceeding to attack synoptic conceptions of history, it is first necessary to be quite definite as to what one
is fighting against and for. One must first examine the nature of man's
standing in the historical processes so as to secure his relative priority
over any process whatever, be it as turbulent and overpowering as it
may. Today more than ever before, it is essential to show itself to be
but one dimension of human existence exhausting neither man's essence
nor his being. The question at isssue is not whether this or that interpretation of the whither and wherefore of history is valid, but whether
the presupposition underlying all comprehensive views, namely that
man can be exhaustively defined in historical terms, is tenable. An
impersonal conception of history is certainly more inclined to obviate
man's nature as a supra-historical being; for as comprehensive, it cannot but swallow up everything it comes across, including the human
being as a whole. There are indications in Berlin's writings that he is
aware of the deeper issues at stake, for they do mention the need for
a new appraisal not only of specific historical theories but also the
status of history itself in the universe at large and in human reality in
particular.

The extent to which Berlin's view constitutes a challenge, a challenge
which may spell a philosophical re-orientation to questions hitherto the
monopoly of existentialist thought, is indicated by his brief discussion
of the origins of the view he is attacking.[7] To his mind, the quest for a
universal, inevitable pattern is spurred by the urge to shake off personal
responsibility, to be absolved from the obligation to deliberate and to
judge, to be free of the sense of accountability to others. Let us not be
judged by others and above all, let us not have to judge ourselves. Let
us escape to the free, impersonal spaces of History and Nature, if we
can no longer find haven in a religious shelter.

It is not by chance that when discussing the hidden source of the
notion of inevitability, and identifying it with the desire to shift the
blame to another, impersonal factor, Berlin reminds us that Mussolini,
when informed that the Allied Forces had landed in Sicily exclaimed:
"History has seized us by the throat...." For Berlin feels that the
question of inevitability is not an "academic" dispute locked safely
away behind gates, but has aroused the response of wide circles of
society. Berlin attributes the popularity of the notion of inevitability
to the same psychological factor which sponsored its introduction,
namely to the urge to shirk responsibility. In this respect his sleight

[7] *Historical Inevitability*, p. 77.

of the hand is reminiscent of the psychological explanations of Fascism current in the various discussions of the issue. Fascism was accounted for as an attempt to shift the blame to some other so that the individual would be absolved from his obligation to shoulder his share of blame. But whereas Fascism was said to shift the blame or the responsibility from the masses to a single leader, the comprehensive conceptions of history are said to have transferred responsibility to the impersonal realm of her Royal, anonymous, omnipotent Highness – History.

It is however still a question whether a psychological argument couched in such modern terms as escapism or shirking, is an exhaustive criticism of a view such as the synoptic theory of history. Still the psychological argument does make the important point that the so-called scientific views are but masks for very unscientific and even irrational drives. This does not mean that Berlin questions the validity of the natural sciences. What he is castigating is the importation of pseudo-scientific methods and goals into the social and historical domains. Even so it might easily be objected that it would be just as logical to trace these views precisely to rational motives. For is not the quest for rationality or the endeavour to reduce the historical course of events to a fixed, permanent pattern, a manifestation of man's basic rationality? Thus the law-abidingness of history is not only possible but actual – manifest in man's very quest for it. It is precisely in history – so the argument might run – as preserving the central processes and passing over the digressiveness and waywardness of the manifold particulars, that man's fundamental rationality is revealed. These law-abiding permanences are the measure of human nature as rational and the quest for them, rather than being a flight from the responsibility inherent in rational conduct, is precisely a search for rationality. If this view is a substitute for religion, it is precisely because it preaches faith in reason. Thus while the argument from psychological origins is important in itself, it does not constitute a convincing philosophical objection. It can at best serve either as a prologue or as an epilogue to a philosophical critique of the notion of inevitability.

One might suggest that from a philosophical point of view the vulnerable point in the synoptic theories of history lies in their failure to cope with the following problem: does the assumption of the law-abidingness or rationality of history necessarily imply that the individual agent is but the object of the historical process? Or does rationality, as a manifestation of the activity of reason, on the contrary prove man's supremacy over all circumstances, natural and historical alike? Rationality is the dividing line between man and the world, be it the given world of nature or the man-made world of history. Man is rational because he is endowed with reason; as such he surpasses the historical process and cannot be exhaustively defined in terms of it. Man's rationality cannot be accounted for historically, since it is an essential determination. As a determination of human essence, rationality transcends history and is prior to it. Hence if one seeks to establish the possibility and actuality of personal responsibility, one must show that it is intrinsically bound up with a creature whose essence history cannot exhaust because he is endowed with reason. History must be explained in terms of human essence and not the other way round. The point of departure of a humanistic conception of history must be man's inalienable priority over his objective circumstances. It is because they indicate a breach with the school of philosophy which is not inclined to consider man with a capital "M", that Berlin's writings are so important. And because Berlin's call for a man-centred conception of history is moderate, cool-headed and free of romantic illusions, it represents an important shift in the current trend of English philosophy: a shift towards a philosophical theory of history which takes into full consideration the moral and, in general, value-permeated aspects of human existence, and conceives of man as an agent and not as a patient only. Berlin is working towards a philosophical world-picture within the framework of which history need not transgress Kant's categorical imperative of the demand that man never be regarded merely as a means but always as an end as well. From the point of view of historical theory the imperative asserts that man should never be merely the object of historical processes, but always their subject as well, and as a subject he is necessarily an agent, responsible and accountable. Here we can trace the roots of the political implications of this theory to be dealt with presently.

Berlin attempts to formulate an historical theory compatible with Kant's categorical imperative. To be sure, Marx sought to integrate the Kantian ethics into his philosophy of history. According to Marx, it is history, as an objective process towards liberty, that will eventually constitute man as a subject. Man is immersed in the process in order to emerge from it a free person, free to develop all his capacities, no longer subjugated by products of his own making, no longer alien to himself, no longer self-alienating. The price man pays in terms of being swept along as an object by the historical process, is worth paying, for it shall buy his future freedom and with freedom, an unassailable, permanent position as subject. The question is, however, whether man can be constituted a subject by being reduced to, and identified with, a process the participation in which costs him his status as subject. Is it only in an eschatological future that that status can be realized? Or is it not rather realized, at least in principle, right now; actual, at least as a potentiality, always and hence also here and now? Rather than assert man's position as a subject to be contingent upon an objective process, is it not more feasible to affirm that only man himself, as potentially a subject from the first, can actualize and guarantee his status as a subject? The only real question is how to guarantee a maximum realization of man's potential subjectness and liberty, and not how man as a subjugated object today can be transmuted into a free subject tomorrow. The grave political and human implications of overlooking man's present status are all too evident. If it is true that man at present is but an object, and that only in the future will he win a subject-status, why then he has only to keep his mouth shut and put himself in the hands of the regime which will, one-day, bring him to the safe harbour of "subjecthood." Now, a man who is an object-for-the-time-being precisely in order that he become a subject in the future, is necessarily a mere object, the object of a regime which has the right to criticize him whereas he, as object, must keep his mouth shut. How could it be otherwise? How can a mere object be critical if criticism is the exercise of the very subject-status? Of course, man can criticize himself if told to by the regime, for in this case self-criticism does not constitute an act of conscience or self-regulation rooted in one's position as subject, but precisely acquiescence to the regime or to the policemen within as representing the regime without. So much for the concrete implications of the presupposition of a so-called gulf between the present state of the historical process and the future state it is to bring about.

Clearly there is a need to determine whether man is a subject by his very essence or whether his status is a gift he will someday receive from the historical process, a gift without which he remains an object. Thus a critique of comprehensive, impersonal historical theories and the insistence upon latitude for personal agency and personal responsibility, are ultimately bound up with man's conception of himself as a creature whose essence is not historically determined but is rather beyond and prior to history. At times history befriends man, at times it besieges him and there is no denying its overwhelming force. All the same, history does not create man. Where the synoptic approach goes wrong is in its failure to distinguish between what is partial, that is, historical, and what is comprehensive or human. Its mistake indicates that it has not grasped the essence of that very rationality it seeks. Instead of seeking the origin of human reason in history, it should rather have sought it in its only source – namely in man himself.[8]

5.

To Berlin's mind, the quest for fixed, immutable historical laws represents an infiltration of the social sciences into the domain of history, or an imitation of the social sciences' imitation of the natural sciences. However, it should be noted that Berlin's criticism of the importation of science into an historical theory is cautious and hence well-taken. He emphasizes the need to take careful account of what the social sciences have revealed. For one thing, they have shown the scope of human choice to be far narrower than we were wont to assume, by indicating those objective factors determining decision and action over which the individual has no control (such as heredity, environment, class, prevailing spiritual climate and so on). For another thing they have called our attention to the fact that when we compare diverse value-frameworks, we are inclined to set up our own (inherited or chosen) system as the immutable, universal one. (See pages 35–36 of *Historical Inevitability*.) The point he is making is that he would by no means have us ignore the impersonal factors studied by science. To insist upon the authority of personal decision and to call upon historical thought to acknowledge its authority, is not to propose that historical action works itself out in a void. In repudiating the theory of inevitable historical laws one does not find oneself soaring like a dove through airless, hence unresisting, empty space – to use Kant's simile. There is no denying the effective presence of the impersonal social field, effective in terms of the restrictions it imposes upon action as well as the objective motives it provides for it. All the same, human existence in all its complexity is not reducible to the social field nor can man's essence and status be exhaustively defined in terms of it. Here Berlin appeals to common sense which does not doubt even for a moment that although man is indeed hedged in on all sides by "objective factors" he is nevertheless a responsible agent. Not that Berlin considers his position proved by common sense. He appeals to common sense only in order to show that man's age-long conviction, based upon

---

[8] Concerning the question, Man – object or subject, see Meshulam Groll, "On Human Dignity", Megamot, Vol. 3/1, 1951, p. 50, Jerusalem (Hebrew). See also the present author's *On the Human Subject, Studies in the Phenomenology of Ethics and Politics*, Springfield, Ill., 1966, pp. 167ff.

actual experience and the wisdom passed down from generation to generation cannot simply be ignored. Yet it has been ignored by the synoptic theories whose assertion of impersonal inevitability stands – as Berlin sees it – in glaring contradiction to the firm conviction of mankind. Because the demand to recognize the right of common sense to be heard is characteristic of the school of thought represented by Berlin we might examine it more fully.

6.

As is well known, England, in its political life, has managed to remove the sting of revolutionary changes by incorporating them into its tradition, the very tradition against which revolutionary steps are taken. This is what happened to Cromwell's revolution which became yet another stage in the evolution of the English way of political life; this is what is happening today to the once warring factions of British philosophy. Thus Reid had attacked Hume's empiricism and its refusal to recognize as true any judgment which could not be based upon sensuous evidence, so as to establish the immunity of those judgments the truth of which is independent of sense-perception, say the judgment that every event has a cause. Today we are witnessing a reconciliation between the rigorist empiricist faction which demands that all beliefs be put to the test of factual evidence and the faction standing up for the rights of those intuitive convictions which need not be put to this test because they are independent of sense-perception. Thus while the demand for "verification of meanings" is still acknowledged, and though the empiricist position is therefore still unshaken, yet its rigorist sting has been removed and common sense is once more acknowledged. Berlin, however is not inclined to approach his problems from a semantic point of view; he takes an emphatically humanistic interest in ethics and politics and obviously does not consider the analytical approach an adequate way of coping with ethical and political problems. True, he does not take explicit exception to what is known as analytical philosophy. Nevertheless, the fact that in his writings he is occupied primarily with historical questions and with the history of ideas, might be taken as an indication of an implicit tendency to break away from the central stream. It is his search for a more adequate approach to historical, ethical and political problems that has led Berlin to have recourse to common-sense as well as to empirical observation. Berlin apparently feels that common sense is itself an empirical fact, inextricably bound up with human experience and which cannot, therefore, be justifiably ignored by historical thought. To his mind, an historical theory which has an explanation for every single occurrence, that has a compartment for every detail in its immutable filing-cabinet, is anti-empirical through and through. Hence it can offer no evidence for its hypothetical unitary, all-embracing pattern comprehending all pheno-mena. This hypothesis is metaphysical because it disdains the evidence of common experience. Berlin does not rest his case with this accusation of anti-empiricism, but calls common sense to the witness-stand, thoroughly convinced that it has every right to be heard and sufficient authority to judge for itself.

Our own good sense (Berlin is apparently referring to professional historians) continues to praise and to blame historical phenomena which we are busily arranging in a fixed, law-abiding framework, a framework which renders evaluation meaningless. Is it possible, Berlin asks, that a normal human being or even a practicing historian, can really be taken in by this curious fairy-tale about an inevitable course of historical events? The authors of this fairy-tale will no doubt remind Berlin that the history of science affords sufficient evidence of theories deemed fantastic by the court of common sense. One need only recall the reception of Copernicus' world-picture, or Galileo's. By now we should have learned not to be discouraged by the prophets of common sense. Moreover it stands to reason that common sense prefers concrete, sensuously presentable world-pictures to nonsensuous, say mathemati-cal ones. Does not common sense rebuke modern art precisely because it is abstract? The inventors of new forms, and with them the histo-rians, can take comfort in the fact that common sense is as hasty to approve as it was to disapprove once the shock of novelty has worn off. Is not psychoanalysis as popular today as it was unpopular just a generation ago? Has not that curious collection of hypothesis, termini-logy and methodology become part and parcel of everyday thought? Is it not obvious that the likes and dislikes of common sense are no test of the validity of a theoretical conception?

Berlin would readily admit all this, for he has recourse to the argu-ment from common sense only in order to present his own interest in tra-ditional philosophical terms, letting common sense speak for him against those who would explain away this interest by means of the intricate machinery of all-inclusive patterns. Precisely because it is unsophisti-cated and unspoiled, common sense can still put the question of perso-nal responsibility without beating around the bush, so to speak. Perhaps in this case the common sense suspicion of novelty which leaves one unimpressed by the argument that these views speak for modern man, is laudable. While common sense is no proof, neither is modernity. Yet although we all hasten to ignore common sense, none of us seems to question the self-evidence of modernity, obviously feeling that if it conflicts with the facts, so much the worse for the facts.

That Berlin objects to modernism is indicated by his statement to the effect that those eighteenth century thinkers who considered the problem of free will a real problem and protested against such interpretations as would explain it away were perfectly right to feel as they did. Professor Ryle expressed the view that the problem of free will is a "natural" philosophical problem, as against "artificial" problems implied in the usage of language. Berlin agrees wholeheartedly with Dr. Johnson who always let his common sense have the last word (see page 27 of the essay *Historical Inevitability*). And it was a moral argument which was put forward in justification of the dogged refusal of common sense to surrender to the casuistic and hair-splitting obviation of the problem of free will. According to Berlin, there is no refuting Kant's assertion that were we not able to do something, we would not be under obligation to do it. From the point of view of historical theory, this implies that were it true that we could not possibly have acted otherwise than we did, we would be responsible neither for our own actions nor *a fortiori* for the course of events. True, Berlin's reading of Kant's statement is quite empirical: for what Kant apparently meant to say was – I am under obligation, therefore I can. My very consciousness of duty bears witness to the fact that I am a creature whose world is not confined to experience, that I am not inextricably enmeshed in the net of mechanical causality, that I am also a citizen of another world, a moral world. This is why Kant believes the empirical self to be determinable by a duty which cannot be accounted for in empirical terms. However, Berlin feels that in dealing with man's historical responsibility it is not enough to show that man is determinable by an obligation which by its very nature transcends history. For duty is actual in history. Thus Berlin transfers Kantian principles from the "pure" moral realm to the empirical sphere of history. The importance of this rendering of Kantian ethics lies also in the fact against the background of linguistic or analytic philosophy Berlin gives moral problems the serious consideration which is their due, and does not relegate them to the sphere of persuasion, as was customary not many years ago, and as is still suggested, though with less certitude and conviction. The very idea put forward in Berlin's writings that historical problems are not unrelated to ethical problems, might perhaps indicate a shift in empiricist thought in general and in posivitism in particular. That the shift is in a backward direction, that is, towards a new recognition of the validity of old ideas, does not detract from its importance. In philosophy, the ideas are always old. Only their formulation and the intellectual conditions under which they return to the fore are new.

To summarize, it would be appropriate to call attention to two observations Berlin makes in *Historical Inevitability*, both of which represent his own point of view: Berlin does not believe that there can be any pat formula to steer us away from the Scylla of peopling the world with great imaginary forces such as the historical forces posited by the comprehensive views of history. Nor, on the other hand, can we find a neat prescription telling us how to steer clear of the Charybdis of confinement to the factual, observable occurrences of this world, that is to empirical conduct determinable by empirical persons at a specific time and place. In other words, the danger is from two directions. On the one side lies the possibility of obviating the reality of the human beings acting in history and of attributing everything to an impersonal course of events; on the other side lies the possibility that we get too involved in the reality of human beings and therefore ignore the broader historical processes in which they play their part. The task of a critical analysis, Berlin adds, is to face these dangers and to navigate its way through the Scylla and the Charybdis to the best of its ability.

The second point Berlin makes is to translate Justice Louis Brandeis' acute observation that the irresistible is often only that which is not resisted, into his own terms. Thus, substituting historical inevitability for irresistibility Berlin remarks that the only ground of the assertion that history is inevitable and hence unimpeachable lies in our own failure to cut ourselves free of its meshes.

Thus we may say that Berlin counters the assertion of the pseudo-inevitability of history by preachers of an all-encompassing historical process with his own call for self-liberation from the pseudo-inevitability of these views. To this mind, the initial step towards self-liberation must be the active resistance to sweeping historical generalizations since these have pulled the wool over many people's eyes, distorting their view of human reality and adding to the public's confusion with respect to the questions of the relation between facts and values and the status of conceptual factors in the natural and the historical sciences respectively.

7.

In the preceding analysis of Collingwood's theory we have seen his attempt to incorporate politics in the framework of his system. Some very obvious difficulties were implied in that attempt. Within the further development of contemporary English philosophy, we see again the connection established between history and the political sphere. Presently it is our task to show the connection inherent in Isaiah Berlin's view; later on we shall find another aspect involved in Michael Oakeshott's view of politics.

Though in Berlin's essay, *Two Concepts of Liberty* we hardly find any clearly expressed statement as to the connection between his criticism of the notion of inevitability in history and the political implications of this criticism in terms of liberty, this connection becomes apparent on closer examination of the text.

"No doubt every interpretation of the word liberty, however unusual, must include a minimum of what I have called 'negative' liberty. There must be an area within which my wishes are not frustrated."[9] Though the universe of discourse of this analysis is the sphere of politics, one can easily assume that were there a sweeping historical-impersonal-inevitable process, there would be no room left for "negative" liberty and thus for personal responsibility. The denial of a historical process with a sweeping rhythm of its own is thus supplemented by the denial of the right of the political realm to eradicate totally the personal sphere. The political aspect is, as it were, the historical process written in small letters. The prevention within the political realm does not take place by impersonal forces of the process, but by human beings who prevent one from attaining his goal.

The assumption of the area safeguarded by negative freedom amounts to the assumption of the personal field. This field in turn is rooted in human nature, which is, as it were, the last refuge of privacy within any sphere governed by its inner logic – "that which a man cannot give up without offending against the essence of his human nature."[10] To be sure, no comprehensive theory of human nature is offered, neither in the analysis of the historical process nor in the analysis of the concept of liberty. But the operative, if we may use this term, impact of human nature is clear: given the existence of spheres with a logic of their own either in terms of history or in terms

---

[9] *Two Concepts of Liberty*, Oxford, 1958, p. 46.
[10] *Ibid.*, p. 11.

of politics, a sphere with a logic of its own exists as well, – a sphere governed by the essentials of human nature. This sphere having an essence of its own cannot be totally submerged in another sphere, given that there are such other spheres as well.

Though no theory of human nature is offered, there is a hint concerning one aspect of human behaviour significant both for the political and the historical spheres alike mentioned before in the analysis of historical inevitability. "If, as I believe, the ends of men are many, and not all of them are in principle compatible with each other, then the possibility of conflict – and of tragedy – can never wholly be eliminated from human life, either personal or social."[11] The assumption of plurality is at least formally connected with the denial of a sweeping process, having one end and one course only. Thus here too the political implications of the view of history become patent. Since the safeguarding of the personal area and concurrently of negative liberty is ultimately rooted in human nature, human nature is bound to be a principle for political action. Thus Berlin, with all due caution, assumes *principles* in the political spheres. "Principles are not less sacred because their duration cannot be guaranteed."[12] And since Collingwood too spoke about barbarism against civilisation we may quote now the dictum mentioned by Berlin: "To realise the relative validity of one's conviction and yet stand for them unflinchingly, is what distinguishes a civilised man from a barbarian."[13]

Turning now to another aspect of contemporary English philosophy related both to history and to politics, we shall easily notice the denial of principles and their validity in the political sphere.

[11] *Ibid.*, p. 54.
[12] *Ibid.*, p. 57.
[13] *Ibid.*

CHAPTER III

HISTORY, TRADITION AND POLITICS:
MICHAEL OAKESHOTT

I.

In the previous pages the connection between politics and history has been brought into relief from different points of view. The difference corresponds to the difference in focus which characterizes the respective system explored. The very term "history" – as we have seen – is used to denote a variety of meanings. In the course of Collingwood's development, the term was made to carry several different connotations; in Isaiah Berlin the term denotes the process in time and its rhythm.

The connection between politics and history is brought into relief from still another point of view in Professor Oakeshott's theory of politics. Here again, the difference in viewpoint corresponds to the difference in focus of Oakeshott's system (if "system" is the proper word to use). Underlying his conception of the relation between politics and history is his distinction between two approaches to the past, the one historical and the other practical. It is noteworthy that he draws this distinction not only in his later writings, where he devotes himself to political questions in particular, but also in his *Experience and its Modes* (1928), where he considers more general problems.

The *genus proximum* of Oakeshott's analysis is the position of the past and our attitude towards the past. Within this framework he uses the term "history" to signify a study of the world *"sub specie praeteritorum."*[1] To Professor Oakeshott's mind, "History is the past for the sake of the past. What the historian is interested in is a dead past; a past unlike the present."[2] In the proper sense of the word, then, "history" connotes a concern with the past for the sake of the past. In its capacity as a concern with the past for its own sake, history entails

---

[1] *Experience and its Modes*, Cambridge, 1933, p. 118.
[2] *Ibid.*, p. 106.

emancipation from the exclusive concern with the present and the activities conducted within the framework of the present. Though he admits that under certain circumstances our concern with the present can utilize the concern with the past, Oakeshott nevertheless draws a clear-cut distinction between the concern with the past for its own sake, and the concern with the present. This distinction may be regarded as a constant factor in Oakeshott's writings. It is to be found not only in *Experience and its Modes*, but also in *Rationalism in Politics*. In the former Oakeshott maintains that "whenever the past is seen in specific relation to the present, the past is not the past in history."[3] while in the latter, "in the specifically 'historical' attitude ... the past is not viewed in relation to the present, and is not treated as if it were present."[4] Both statements imply that an historical concern with the past entails emancipation from the exclusive concern with the present.

This emancipation, however, does not involve a total severance of the ties between past and present. What it does involve is an orientation to the present not for its own sake but for the sake of explaining it in terms of the past. To put it another way, the historian's emancipation from exclusive concern with the present entails a shift of interest from the present *qua* the dimension in which we must act, to the present *qua* the dimension of events which we must explain. Hence, so the argument runs, "among those who regard present events as evidence for events that have already taken place, 'the historian' is taken to be supreme. ... The activity of the historian is pre-eminently that of understanding present events – the things that are before him – as evidence for past happenings."[5]

This definition of the historian's activity warrants the conclusion that, understood properly, history as concerned with the past proper, involves a theoretical attitude and consequently cannot serve as a starting-point for an analysis of the nature of politics. A historical concern with the past is excluded from the political universe of discourse by the very nature of history. Properly understood, history is a mode of experience in its own right. Partial though this mode of experience may be, it is self-enclosed in its partiality.

---

[3] *Ibid.*, p. 105.
[4] "The Activity of Being an Historian", in *Rationalism in Politics and other Essays*, London, 1962, p. 154.
[5] *Ibid.*, p. 150.

2.

History, like science, involves an attitude of detachment. Consequently, an historical attitude towards the past consists in "emancipation from the primordial and once almost exclusive practical attitude of mankind."[6] Here we have advanced from the *genus proximum* of Professor Oakeshott's analysis, viz. the concern with the past, to the *differentia specifica* which distinguishes the historical attitude towards the past from the practical attitude towards it. So radical does the difference between these attitudes seem to Oakeshott, that he presents it not merely as a difference in subjective approach, but even as a difference in logical position. According to him, "Practice" and "History" are two logically distinct universes of discourse."[7]

The historical and the practical attitudes differ from one another in several aspects. But all the differences between them are ultimately reducible to the basic distinction between observation and action. The end of history, i.e. of a concern with the past for its own sake, is not action but observation. The end of practice, by contrast, is not observation but action. In practice, as Oakeshott observes, "alteration of existence is undertaken ... It is both the production and the prevention of change, and in either case it is not merely a programme for action, but action itself."[8] The primary distinguishing mark which differentiates the practical attitude from the historical one, may accordingly be defined as follows: "In practical experience reality is asserted under the category of change."[9]

By virtue of its orientation to change, the practical attitude is related not to the subject matter of history – the past – but to the agent and his motives. Whereas history views the world "*sub specie praeteritorum,*" practice views the world "*sub specie voluntatis.*"[10] It is true that orientation to change may take the form of an attempt to utilize the past for the sake of the present, in which case practice seems to be concerned with the subject-matter of history, i.e. with the past. But the distinction between the historical and practical attitudes to this subject-matter still remains. And what counts is not the subject-matter itself but the attitude towards it.

This is what Oakeshott has in mind when he writes: "Whenever the

[6] *Ibid.*
[7] See *ibid.*, p. 164.
[8] *Experience and its Modes*, p. 25.
[9] *Ibid.*, p. 273.
[10] Cf. *ibid.*, p. 258.

present is sought in the past, and whenever the past is regarded as merely a refuge from the present, the past involved is a practical, and not an historical past."[11] In other words, he maintains that "if we understand a past event merely in relation to ourselves and our own current activities, our attitude may be said to be a 'practical attitude'."[12]

In the light of Oakeshott's distinction between history and practice in terms of their respective approaches to the past, we can understand his conception of the relation between history and politics. For according to him, a practical attitude towards the past is an essential constituent of the political attitude towards the past. "The practical past," he writes, "will be found, in general, to serve either of two masters – politics or religion ... this political past, our past as ours, is not, as such the historical past."[13] Putting the same point more bluntly, Oakeshott argues that if a man "is a politician, he approves whatever in the past appears to support his political predilections and denounces whatever is hostile to them."[14]

If the politician's attitude to the past is essentially practical, then his attitude – unlike the historian's – entails no explanation of the events towards which he orients himself. "There is no specifically 'practical' explanation of anything: the word 'politics' stands for holding certain kinds of actions and thinking in terms of certain practical, not explanatory, considerations."[15]

Having pointed out the systematic distinction upon which Oakeshott's approach to the relation between history and politics is based, let us now turn to examine his conception of politics.

3.

To begin with, it should be noted that the *genus proximum* of political activity is not history proper, but a relatedness to the course of events which flows from past to present. For, understood in the proper sense of an attitude which entails emancipation from practice, history cannot constitute a source of political conduct. But if by relatedness to the past one implies relatedness to tradition, then one can claim that this mode of relatedness to the past plays a central role in the political

---

[11] *Ibid.*, p. 103.
[12] "The Activity of Being an Historian", *ibid.*, p. 147.
[13] *Experience and its Modes*, p. 103.
[14] "The Activity of Being an Historian", in *Rationalism in Politics*, pp. 153–154.
[15] "The Study of 'Politics' in a University", *ibid.*, p. 327.

sphere. For tradition – or the cumulative deposit of experience of the generations and the firmly established, persistent patterns of conduct – can be understood as that element of the past which intervenes and plays a regulative role in the present.

How can the position occupied by tradition in the political sphere be explained? Obviously, the explanation lies not in history, but in political activity as a particular manifestation of the practical attitude in general.

A relatedness to tradition pertains to the definition of politics: "Politics I take to be the activity of attending to the general arrangements of a set of people whom chance or choice have brought together ... I speak of this activity as 'attending to arrangements' rather than as 'making arrangements'."[16] Oakeshott then defines politics as a mode of activity concerned with men's life in common. His definition does not specify the particular aspects of men's life in common which constitute the proper concern of politics. In other words, he fails to include in his definition of politics the projection and crystallization of power which distinguishes men's political life (proper) in common from, e.g., their social life in common. While the definition he proposes may indicate the *genus proximum* of politics, it clearly omits the *differentia specifica*. This omission is not to be regarded merely as a terminological abbreviation. It should rather be conceived as symptomatic of Oakeshott's basic approach, which will be examined presently.

As an activity of "attending to the general arrangements of a set of people," politics goes hand in hand with governing. That Oakeshott does not clarify the precise nature of the relation between the activity of politics and the activity of governing, follows from his definition of the latter. "Governing," he writes, "is a specific and limited activity, namely the provision and custody of general rules of conduct, which are understood, not as plans for imposing substantive activities, but as instruments enabling people to pursue the activities of their own choice."[17] Governing, then, presupposes that the people who are engaged in political activity share certain beliefs in common. These beliefs are neither created nor even crystallized by the activity of governing. In this respect, governing is analogous to the trend of linguistic philosophy which does not construct, but only analyses, the ideas, concepts, opinions etc., which constitute its subject-matter. Or, to use Oakeshott's own analogy, "the office of government is merely to

---

16 "Political Education", *ibid.*, p. 112.
17 "On Being Conservative", *ibid.*, p. 184.

rule. .... The image of the ruler is the umpire whose business is to administer the rules of the game, or the chairman who governs the debate according to known rules but does not himself participate in it."[18]

Underlying the opinion that governing does not involve creative intervention in the social set-up, is the idea of government as a passive policeman. That Oakeshott recognizes this trend of his political philosophy is witnessed by his allusions to the idea of government as concerned with, and only with, those activities which are liable to conflict and clash with one another.[19] These allusions do not specify what the relation of government to such activities involves. Whether the task of government is to eliminate the causes of conflict, or whether its task is only to propose *ad hoc* solutions to clashes which have actually occurred or are about to occur, is a question which Oakeshott leaves open. But his comparison of the ruler to the umpire and the chairman indicates that he would choose the latter alternative and assign the ruler the task of resolving conflicts rather than removing their cause.

The ruler, Oakeshott maintains, "does not suppose that the office of government is to do nothing. As he understands it, there is a work to be done only in virtue of a genuine acceptance of current beliefs simply because they are current, and current activities simply because they are afoot."[20] Thus the explanation for the fact that the government does not interfere in the social setting, lies in the government's obligation to accept current beliefs and activities simply because they are current. The relation between the three factors – politics, government, and prevalent beliefs and activities – might accordingly be described as follows: Current views and activities provide politics with the raw material which it must shape. Politics, in turn, provides government with the crystallized codes and patterns of conduct which it must accept.

This conception of politics as an activity of "attending to" arrangements, rather than an activity of "making" arrangements, explains Oakeshott's assertion that "politics is not a science of setting up a permanently impregnable society; it is the art of knowing what to do next in promotion of an already existing traditional type of society."[21] What remains to be explained is the reason for including a time-determination ("next") in his definition of politics. Is he simply rationalizing

[18] *Ibid.*, p. 187.
[19] Cf. *ibid.*, p. 189.
[20] *Ibid.*, p. 188.
[21] "The Political Economy of Freedom", *ibid.*, p. 58.

the attitude of "wait and see" or of "muddling through?" To answer
this question it is necessary to expose the tacit presuppositions of his
definition of politics in terms of a limited time-horizon. To do so we
must recur to his correlation of politics with tradition.

Being by definition an activity of "attending to the general arrangements of a set of people," and consequently an activity which presupposes that those arrangements are given, politics obviously cannot be
construed as an activity capable of establishing a society. Politics
cannot create the common codes and patterns of conduct which it
presupposes as given. For a society cannot be created without going
beyond tradition, i.e. without going beyond the given facts of politics.
In so far as he proceeds on this assumption, Oakeshott obviously does
not distinguish between society and state. His use of the same term,
"general arrangements," when describing both the body-social and the
body-politic, seems to imply that he dismisses as meaningless the distinction upon which the traditional theories of a social contract are
based. For the purpose of those theories is to explain the difference between the body-social and the body-politic. At any rate, he apparently
presumes that politics presupposes the body-politic.

That the issue here is not merely a matter of terminology follows
from Oakeshott's broad definition of political activity in terms of
"general arrangements." For this definition, as we have seen, omits the
differentia specifica in virtue of which the state differs from other col-
lective forms of men's life in common. The point to be borne in mind,
however, is that Oakeshott's confinement of politics within a restricted
time-span, excludes from the very definition of political activity the
creative or utopian element. To explain this point it is necessary to
consider more closely the implications of Oakeshott's conception of
tradition.

4.

As we have seen, Oakeshott uses the term "tradition" to denote the
accumulated experience of the generations. Understood in this sense,
the concept of tradition carries no political connotations. But if one
correlates the idea of accumulation with the idea of a continuous,
gradual process, then one can suggest a political connotation of tradition. From a political viewpoint, this might be called the liberal
element in tradition; while from a philosophical viewpoint, it might be
called the historicist element in tradition. Be this as it may, the point

is that accumulation necessarily consists in a process of gradual growth, i.e. in an evolutionary process. Underlying Oakeshott's correlation of tradition with evolution and continuity, is the idea of experience as a non-conceptual, practical, and common-sense activity.

Understood in this sense, the idea of experience underlying Oakeshott's conception of tradition differs from the idea of experience expounded in his *Experience and its Modes*. This is not to overlook that he invokes his earlier idea when criticizing the empiricist view of experience,[22] but to imply that it would be difficult to reconcile his idea of experience with his idea of politics as a short-range activity by its very definition. If the function of the experience-concept is to unify data in the manner of a scientific hypothesis, then the range of experience cannot be restricted by any time-determination. The function of a scientific hypothesis is not merely to control the "next" experiment conducted in the laboratory. Nor can a scientific hypothesis be confined, from the outset, within the limits of a fixed time-span. In any event, Oakeshott's theory presents experience as a synthetic entity in which practical knowledge and a theoretical concept figure in combination.

To put it another way, Oakeshott uses the term "experience" in the Aristotelian sense of knowledge acquired from one's ancestors, rather than in the scientific sense of knowledge acquired from one's personal confrontation with, and control of, one's actual circumstances. Given this use of the term "experience," we can understand his tendency to correlate tradition with inheritance, or else with a balanced relationship between past, present, and future, with continuity and consensus, etc. The non-conceptual character of tradition *qua* cumulative experience finds prominent reflection in the relation between a traditional society and its individual members. This relation is embodied in education in general, and in political education in particular.

According to Oakeshott, education is not a purposeful activity; for, "living as a member of association is always an education in motive."[23] Being practical, political knowledge "can neither be thought nor learned but only imparted and acquired, ... and the only way to acquire it is by apprenticeship to a master."[24] Oakeshott goes even further and criticizes the "illusion that politics (can ever be) anything more than the pursuit of intimations; a conversation, not an argu-

---

[22] "Political Education", *ibid.*, p. 113.
[23] Review of J. D. Mabboth's "The State and the Citizen", *Mind*, Vol. LVIII/231, 1949, p. 389.
[24] "Rationalism in Politics", *ibid.*, p. 11.

ment.''[25] These statements clearly underline the non-conceptual connotation of tradition and bring into relief its non-intellectual, or even
behaviouristic implications. For they present politics as inherent in
men's patterns of conduct and suggest that commitment to these
patterns of conduct is produced by these very patterns.

The Aristotelian motif in Oakeshott's thought is very significant. It
implies that political activity is oriented not to abstractions but to
institutions. But from the concern of politics with institutions, Oakeshott draws the far-reaching conclusion that the province of politics is
limited to those institutions which already exist. Politics can accommodate no design, no attempt to transcend the given institutional
setting, unless that design and that attempt grow out of the tradition
of the existing institutions. The existence of those institutions cannot
be challenged; it can only be continued.

Though he discusses the relation between continuity and change,
Oakeshott recognizes the legitimacy of only such changes as are out-
growths of continuity itself. In his theory, tradition is conceived as a
biological entity with the power of self-regulation, i.e. with the ability
to sustain, by itself, an internal balance among the temporal dimensions
and between the temporal dimensions and the various factors which
are related to them. Thus tradition becomes the force whereby society
is integrated. Now, this line of reasoning is somewhat circular. Taking
its departure from the existence of a traditional society, it concludes
(a) that tradition plays a crucial part in the existence of society; and
(b) that the transcendence of tradition entails the transcendence of the
existing society.

In addition to being somewhat circular, Oakeshott's trend of thought
is also rather dogmatic. Though in his explicit statements he seems to
tend towards an organic and cumulative view, his latent thought-
process seems to be controlled by a categorial dichotomy between tradition and utopian design. To see that this is so, one need only consider
some of the questions with which Oakeshott does not deal. One such
question is, How does utopian design affect short-range political policy?
Or, to take a concrete example, how does the project of e.g. nationali-
zation affect the programme for action in any particular span of time?
Another question is, What are the consequences of an encounter between a particular political tradition and a universalistic utopian
design? How does the quasi-external element of utopian design alter

[25] "Political Education", *ibid.*, p. 125.

the tradition? And how does the tradition give meaning to the utopian design?

Concerning these questions, Oakeshott's standpoint might be called pragmatic, in the sense that it rests upon *de facto* results. To his mind, a clear-cut dichotomy between tradition and utopian design exists from the outset. If a utopian design manages to overcome the inertia of tradition, the penetration of tradition by design results in the absorption of the design into the tradition. Thus the initially external element becomes virtually internal. The question, however, is why one must regard that tradition which has been penetrated – *de facto* – by design, as the antithesis of utopian design. To illustrate the point we can use the examples brought by Oakeshott, namely the establishment of a society upon the declaration of the Rights of Man, and the Education Act of 1944. In both cases an extra-traditional design is executed in actual fact. In one case execution results in the creation of a new tradition; in the other case, execution supplements the existing tradition. From these examples Oakeshott draws the twofold conclusion that (a) the index of a utopian act's success is its becoming tradition; and that (b) the index of a utopian act's failure is its certification as an extra-traditional act.

5.

At this juncture it is appropriate to remark that the content and implications of Oakeshott's concept of tradition, as well as the difficulties with which it is faced, are strikingly similar to the content and implications of Savigny's concept of *Volksgeist* and the difficulties with which it is attended. Like Savigny's *Volksgeist*, Oakeshott's tradition is at once an existing fact and a regulative force, a fact and a value. Being a value, tradition – like *Volksgeist* – cannot be deliberately altered without being damaged. In relation to tradition, change is not only a non-value but even an anti-value. This follows of necessity from the value-framework in which the concept of tradition is anchored; for in that framework, continuous accumulation is the supreme value.

It is therefore no wonder that a deep distrust of utopianism is an important article of Oakeshott's *credo*. His distrust derives partly from recent historical experience, partly from pragmatic considerations, and partly from theoretical considerations. It is probably recent experience or attempts to impose utopian visions upon political reality which prompts him to maintain that "the conjunction of dreaming and ruling generates tyranny.''[26] Pragmatic considerations lead him to weigh the disadvantages, as well as the advantages of deliberate alteration and to conclude that, "innovation entails certain loss and possible gain. Therefore, the onus of proof, to show that the proposed change may be expected to be on the whole beneficial, rests with the would-be innovator.''[27] The same pragmatic considerations underly his favourable estimate of the conservative attitude, as the antidote to utopianism: "To be conservative" he maintains, "is to prefer the familiar to the unknown, to prefer the tried to the untried, past to mystery, the actual to the possible, the limited to the unbounded, the near to the distant, the sufficient to the superabundant, the convenient to the perfect, present laughter to utopian bliss.''[28]

As for the theoretical considerations behind Oakeshott's distrust of utopian design, these may be traced to his biological interpretation of tradition. It is this interpretation which leads him to remark "that the more closely innovation resembles growth (that is, the more clearly it is intimated in, and not merely imposed upon, the situation), the less likely it is to result in a preponderance of loss.''[29] Oakeshott's attitude to utopianism may accordingly be said to consist in a combination of skepticism with faith: skepticism as to the practical advantage of deliberate innovation imposed from without, faith in the process of growth if left to itself.

Still another aspect of Oakeshott's attitude can be brought into relief by looking back at his *Experience and its Modes* from the perspective of his political thought. Political utopia is presented there as a constructive and constructed image of a given state of affairs. The purpose of a political utopia is to consider practical activities from a position which is not *of* practice but *above* it. And the utopian procedure consists in the replacement of practice and experience by abstraction and speculation. The immediate butt of Oakeshott's critical shafts is not utopia but philosophy. But utopianism, as we shall see, is wounded through the sides of philosophy.

Oakeshott formulates his criticism of philosophy in such statements as the following: "Philosophic life is not less a monstrosity than a philosophic science or a philosophic history. Philosophy can and must supersede practical experience; but it cannot take its place.''[30] "To

---

[26] "On Being Conservative", *ibid.*, p. 194.
[27] *Ibid.*, p. 172.
[28] *Ibid.*, p. 169.
[29] *Ibid.*, p. 172.
[30] *Experience and its Modes*, p. 354.

turn philosophy into a way of life is at once to have abandoned life and philosophy. Philosophy is not the enhancement of life, it is the denial of life ... We should listen to philosophers only when they talk philosophy."[31] Now, the censure of utopia implicit in those statements is obviously more withering than the censure of philosophy which they explicitly convey. Philosophy is disparaged only when it oversteps the limits of its proper province – the analysis of experience – and invades the province of life. Provided it knows its place, philosophy does not provoke Oakeshott's disapprobation. Utopia, by contrast, is decried *a limine*; for – so Oakeshott feels – it has no proper province to speak of. Utopia as such is a transgressor, a construction which invades actuality and disrupts the process of its organic growth. By its very nature, utopia usurps the place of life. Philosophy, on the other hand, usurps the place of life not by its very nature, but by perversion of its nature.

What is important to note is the line of reasoning which prompts Oakeshott to decry both philosophy and utopia. For this line of reasoning is still another symptom of the anti-speculative, and biological at that, trend of his thought. His adherence to the philosophy of growth obliges him to oppose the philosophy which strives to guide and control human activities. In fact, he opposes any system of ideas, be it even political, which is subservient to the aims of controlling the present, projecting the future, and criticizing the elevation of facts, as facts, to the rank of values. For all his avowed relativism, or – as he calls it – skepticism, Oakeshott holds an adamantly anti-relativistic view which presents perpetuation as the sole value. This aspect of his approach to the relation between politics and tradition can be clarified by an analysis of the polemical concepts implicit in his theory.

6.

In keeping with his tendency to think in categorial dichotomies, Oakeshott sets up "rationalism" and its sociological expression, planning, as the polar opposite of politics which grows out of a society's tradition. Underlying this opposition is the antithesis between philosophy and tradition, which antithesis should therefore be considered

---

[31] *Ibid.*, p. 355. It is not out of place to mention here the characteristic reservation against utopianism present in a previous stage of English philosophy and indeed in a trend different from that represented by M. Oakeshott. We refer here to J. S. Mill – and indeed to Bentham as well. Mill says that he did not think the utopian doctrines – Owenite, St. Simonian – to be true or desire that they should be acted on. Mill wanted that the higher classes "might be made to see that they had more to fear from the poor when uneducated, than when educated" (J. S. Mill, *Autobiography*, Oxford, 1935, p. 146). Utopias are to be eye-openers.

first. Oakeshott claims that "in general, constitutional tradition is a good substitute for philosophy."[32] The question is: What warrants his presentation of philosophy and constitutional tradition as approaches of equal rank which compete with one another for the self-same human function? The answer seems to be that like philosophy, tradition – as the integrating force of society – constitutes an all-embracing framework. But this answer leaves out of account the crucial difference between the comprehensiveness of tradition and the comprehensiveness of philosophy. No matter how all-embracing it is, the world outlook embodied in a tradition is confined within the limits of a particular social unit or, as Oakeshott puts it, a particular "set of people." By contrast, the world outlook embodied in a philosophy tends towards universality, and is all-embracing in the sense that it can engage any individual or group.

It is true that in another context, Oakeshott discusses the tendency of various political ideologies to transcend the limits of the society in which they originated and to become universal ideologies.[33] The question, however, is how a body of ideas which is particular by definition can become universal. Be the answer what it may, there is a patent difference between the all-embracing particularity of tradition and the all-embracing universality of philosophy. Nevertheless, Oakeshott maintains that within the limits of a given society, tradition is as all-embracing as philosophy. And within those limits, his argument runs, tradition has a clear advantage over philosophy. Being embodied in concepts, philosophy transcends actual experience; being embodied in institutions and patterns of conduct, tradition inheres in, and nurtures actual experience. Hence the value a society sets on philosophy may be regarded as an acid test of its state of health. As evidence that philosophy is, as it were, a compensation for the deprivations of actual or practical life, Oakeshott adduces the fact that "Germans are the only European people which did start more or less with a blank sheet and became philosophers before they had learned how to live."[34]

The antithesis between tradition and philosophy finds reflection in the antithesis between two moral attitudes: one conceives of moral life as a habit of emotion and behaviour rather than as a habit of mind; the other conceives of morality as a reflective application of a moral criterion. The latter attitude "appears in two common varieties: as

---

[32] "Contemporary British Politics", *The Cambridge Journal*, Vol. I/8, 1947–1948, p. 476.
[33] See the "Introduction" to *The Social and Political Doctrines of Contemporary Europe*, Cambridge and New York, 1942, p. XIII.
[34] "The Universities", *The Cambridge Journal*, Vol. II/9, 1948–1949, p. 528.

the self-conscious pursuit of moral ideas and the reflective observance
of moral values."[35] According to Oakeshott, the crisis of Western
Civilization is due to the fact that "our moral life has come to be domi-
nated by the pursuit of ideals ... we have come to think of this domi-
nance as a benefit."[36] To his mind, then, the preponderance of the
reflective attitude is in itself a sign of a crisis in human existence.
Where reflective patterns of actual conduct prevail and shape men's
character, reflection is superfluous. Unlike Hegel, who regarded reflection as a mark of maturity, Oakeshott regards reflection as a sign
of deterioration not only in the political sphere but also in human
civilization and human existence.

Because he identifies philosophy with "rational" philosophy, Oakeshott is able to translate the opposition between tradition and philosophy into an opposition between tradition and rationalism. To understand the latter antithesis, it is necessary to note, (a) that Oakeshott's
use of the term "rationalism" is ambiguous; and (b) that the ambiguity
is due to the intermingling of two distinct meanings with which the
concept of "reason" is associated. The term "reason" can be used to
denote either the faculty of principles (which is roughly the sense in
which St. Thomas and Kant used the term); or a source of techniques
(which is the sense in which programming uses the term). At times
Oakeshott seems to use the term "reason" to denote a faculty of
principles. But by principles he means rules of human behaviour and
not rules of human thought, i.e. moral ideals, not speculative ideas.
When he uses the term "reason" in this sense, he thinks of rationalism
as a tendency to posit moral ideals in the capacity of guiding principles
of human life.

At other times Oakeshott uses the term "reason" to denote a source
of techniques, and accordingly presents rationalism as a tendency to
propose various technical devices as means of implementing principles.
Though he apparently opposes both manifestations of rationalism,
Oakeshott aims most of his critical shafts against the technical form
of rationalistic politics. His opposition to rationalistic politics in the
form of a deliberate pursuit of definite moral ideals is based upon the
tendency of ideals to inspire criticism of reality. And, to his mind,
"*ceaseless* criticism never did anyone or anything any good; it unnerves
the individual and distracts the institutions."[37] What Oakeshott means

---

[35] "The Tower of Babel", *Rationalism in Politics*, p. 66.
[36] *Ibid.*, p. 79.
[37] "The Universities", p. 524.

to imply is not that all criticism of tradition is undesirable, but that the only desirable criticism there of is self-criticism. He assumes, in other words, that tradition contains within itself not only the power of continuity but also the power of criticism. Though he does not explain how this is possible, Oakeshott assumes that a balance between continuity and criticism is desirable and asserts, dogmatically, that both factors are contained within tradition.

Hence he posits an antithesis between "ceaseless criticism" and self-criticism of tradition, and correlates the former with the deliberate pursuit of ideals. The correlation of ceaseless criticism with the pursuit of ideals is sound, since both are moral activities which involve a comparison of reality with something that transcends actual reality. The problem, however, is whether reality can be comprehended altogether without transcending it. Even Oakeshott admits that an hypothesis is the prerequisite of grasping experience. He should therefore have considered the question as to how the moral aspect of human life could be grasped without going beyond what is actually given. As a methodological solution to this question, it might be proposed that in the moral sphere an ideal can fulfill the same function that an hypothesis fulfills in the theoretical sphere – with due allowance for the difference between the moral and theoretical attitudes towards reality. Unless we confine ourselves within the limits of reality as it is given, we cannot justifiably ignore the status occupied by the moral ideal not only in the moral sphere but also in the political sphere.

Oakeshott apparently assumes that there is no difference between the moral ideal and the belief that its realization is possible. This is why he emphasizes the rationalistic implication of the belief in progress and perfectibility. Historically regarded, his observation is certainly correct. The belief that (a) men are rational, and that (b) their very ability to understand and to formulate rational principles bears witness to their power of realizing the idea – this belief pertains to the historical essence of rationalism. But one must distinguish between the historical essence of rationalism and its conceptual essence. There is no necessary connection between transcendence of reality towards a moral ideal (the conceptual essence of rationalism), and the alteration of reality in conformity to the demands of the ideal (the historical essence of rationalism). A reflective moral attitude is not necessarily a naïve one. On the contrary, to be meaningful a reflective moral attitude must not only formulate moral ideals and obligations, but must also recognize the moral gap between the ideal and the real, the "ought" and the "is."

In any event, one must admit that if a practical danger lurks in cease-less criticism, a moral danger lurks in inert continuity.

So much for Oakeshott's objections to rationalism in the form of a deliberate pursuit of moral ideals. Let us now examine his objections to rationalism in the form of a deliberate attempt to solve political problems. According to Oakeshott, the very idea that human life pre-sents problems to be solved is a symptom of the rationalistic attitude. The question here is whether or not there are aspects of human life which call for conscious consideration. Even if we agree to call those aspects "predicaments" instead of "problems," and thus to give the issue a more existentialist resonance, we are still confronted with the question whether or not such predicaments as poverty, disease, igno-rance, old age, unemployment, etc. contain in themselves their own remedies, if not resolutions.

Human predicaments can be dealt with in only one of two ways. Either we think of human life as a river upon which we float slowly, surely and safely to a predestined shore; or we think of human life as a river whose flow is obstructed by shoals and reefs which must be perceived to be circumvented. If we adopt the latter outlook, then we can either count on life's current to carry us safely beyond those shoals and reefs, or steer our own course to safety. To put it non-parabolically, if we grant that life has its problems or predicaments, then we can either hope that they carry their own solutions, or propose solutions of our own. Only a supra-rationalistic view can assume the power of predicaments to resolve themselves; for this assumption posits as the trustworthy guide of human life a *Weltgeist* in a traditional guise, rather than a tradition in the strict sense of the word. Paradoxically enough, Oakeshott's anti-rationalistic argument lays the ground-work for a supra-rationalistic view.

Moreover, Oakeshott fails to see that there is a third form of ratio-nalistic politics which is at equal remove from the supra-rationalistic form implied by his anti-rationalistic argument and the pseudo-rationalistic form derided in his parody of rationalistic politics as a technique of reasoning in a vacuum. This third form of rationalistic politics, which might be called *maieutic* (in the Socratic sense), consists in a deliberate effort to regulate issues which arise with the aid of active understanding – without presuming that their ultimate and final so-lution has been, or can be, found. There is nothing pejoratively abstract about this form of rationalistic politics; it clearly has some bearing upon the actual conduct of social and political life. Unlike supra-rationalistic politics, *maieutic* politics do not assume a self-guiding tradition, or a self-sustaining constitutional balance among the various forces operative in the political sphere. Unlike supra-rationalistic politics, *maieutic* politics are not subservient to the sole end of helping that balance sustain itself, but rather aim at establishing a framework which can accommodate alterations in the distribution of forces called for by particular situations which arise and their prominent issues. If the prominent issue at stake in a particular situation is the very status of society in relation to the sovereign, then it may be necessary to elevate the status of the legislative arm of government. Or if, to take another example, the prominent issue at stake in a particular situation is the welfare of society and its individual members, then it may be necessary to invest the executive arm with regulative power.

"To begin everything *de novo*" is not the function of rationalism in politics. Oakeshott can claim that it is, only because he regards rationalism as an activity of principles conducted in a vacuum. Now, only rationalism in pure logic might perhaps be regarded as an activity of this kind. But rationalism in politics is evidently not an activity conducted in a vacuum; it is an activity conducted in a socio-political setting. *Maieutic* politics involve active intervention in the "arrangements" of society and state; they do not involve abstraction from circumstances because relatedness to circumstances is their reason for being. Consequently to immunize people, through political education, against the contagious infection of rationalism, is to immunize them against politics.

A tendency to abstraction is not the worst fault Oakeshott finds in rationalistic politics. A more obnoxious fault is suggested by the following statement: "To the Liberal and the Catholic mind alike the notion that man can authoritatively plan and impose a way of life upon a society appears to be a piece of pretentious ignorance; it can be entertained only by men who have no respect for human beings and are willing to make them the means to the realization of their own ambition."[38]

The obvious answer to this accusation is that it is a *non sequitur*. There is no necessary connection between planning and an ulterior motive to fulfill personal ambitions. Would Oakeshott accuse Robert Owen, for instance, of personal ambition and of disrespect for human beings? Would he suspect that the "rights of man" or "natural

---

[38] "Introduction" to *The Social and Political Doctrines of Contemporary Europe*, p. XXIII, note.

rights" is an idea which sprang full flown in the megalomaniac imagination of some mysterious individual? Would he not rather admit that it is an outgrowth of a time-honoured tradition – not his tradition, to be sure, but a tradition nonetheless? Were we to assume that this impersonal idea was imposed upon men in order to use them as the means to the realization of personal ambition, we could never uncover the mysterious manner in which wicked men create a worthy tradition. The mystery could be solved only by assuming a *creatio ex nihilo*, i.e. by assuming a beginning and not a tradition.

The circularity of Oakeshott's attack against rationalism in politics can be brought into relief by the following paraphrase of its twofold argument: (a) to constitute the antithesis of planned politics, tradition must be self-regulating and, consequently, supra-rationalistic; (b) to preclude the possibility of planned interference in human affairs, the essential wickedness of man must be taken for granted. Supra-rationalistic tradition renders rationalism superfluous; human wickedness renders it pointless.

7.

Having criticized the particular concepts which control the trend of Oakeshott's theory, we may turn now to an examination of his general assumptions.

(1) For all his explicit statements to the contrary, both in *Experience and its Modes* and in his political writings, Oakeshott believes in the political bearing of principles. One gathers as much from remarks such as the following: "It is safe to say that politics which did not embody a genuine love for erring human beings and even a delight in their endearing stupidities (as well as a desire to relieve society, with the aid of scientific and other knowledge, from some of the consequences of error and stupidity), would be evil."[39] Doesn't this remark bear witness to an acknowledgement of a principle, and a "rationalistic" principle at that? Does it not reflect an explicit evaluation of politics by reference to a moral standard? It is true that the passage quoted ends on a characteristically skeptical note with the remark "that everything in the world is a necessary evil." Nevertheless it seems safe to assume that Oakeshott would probably regard politics guided by a principle of love as a lesser evil than politics guided by a principle of hate.

It follows that at least part of the world is amenable to alteration;

[39] "Science and Society", *The Cambridge Journal*, Vol. I/11, 1947–1948, p. 691.

for man can choose to shape politics in conformity to the love-principle. Being a principle, genuine love for human beings inspires not only toleration and forgiveness of their faults, but also a desire and effort to relieve them from the consequences of their faults by active intervention in their situation. Thus one does not have to share the rationalistic belief that men are essentially rational creatures in order to believe that men's affairs should be "arranged" by reference to a moral standard, Nor, consequently, is it necessary to share the rationalistic belief in order to adopt a reflective attitude towards the arrangement of men's affairs.

Freedom is another principle which Oakeshott acknowledges as pregnant with political implications. It is his fear lest human life be robbed of its freedom that makes him mistrust rationalistic politics in the form of centralized planning. In other words, the object of his mistrust is not rational politics governed by principles but rational politics governed by *certain* principles; for it is the latter which he regards as a threat to freedom. It turns out, then, that the alternative contemplated by Oakeshott is not, either "bookish" principles or tradition; but, either this set of principles or that set of principles.

(2) In his Introduction to Hobbes' *Léviathan*, Oakeshott uses the plural form of the term "tradition". The concept connoted by the term bears the same formal distinguishing marks as it does in *Rationalism in Politics;* but its material implication is different. For here Oakeshott explicitly refers to a tradition of political thought wherein the state is presented as a product of Will and Artifice.[40] The tradition referred to might very well be a "rationalistic" one, considering the fact that deliberate interference in a given state of affairs has been presented as the primary distinguishing mark of rationalism.[41] If Oakeshott regards this conception of the state as legitimate in itself and as the source of a tradition in political thought, then how can he justifiably ignore such a historical manifestation of rationalism as the establishment of a state *de novo*, or the foundation of a regime upon the idea of natural rights? Does he assume the existence of two totally distinct trends, one in the history of political thought whose abstract nature can accommodate rationalism, and one in the history of politics whose concrete character cannot accommodate rationalism?

(3) Oakeshott's theory is characterized by a marked tendency to-

[40] Cf. p. XII of his edition of Hobbes' *Leviathan*, Oxford, 1946.
[41] Following Professor Oakeshott's terminology, A. P. d'Entrèves refers to Hobbes as a 'rationalist'. See *Natural Law: An Introduction to Legal Philosophy*, London, 1951.

wards historicism and relativism. As an example of this tendency one
can cite his survey of the different meanings which the concept of freedom takes on in various political traditions.[42] As another example one
can cite his contention that Liberalism and Nazism are equally legitimate
since both are traditional ideologies, and since traditions as such are
legitimate.[43] If Oakeshott finds Liberalism preferable to Nazism, it is
partly because it is not "the hasty product of a generation" but rather
belongs "to a long and impressive tradition of thought."[44] In other
words, he apparently assumes that the very time-span taken up by
a tradition is an argument in its favour, as if to say that no such argument is afforded by its content. If facts are values, then the larger
the fact, the greater its value.

The question, however, is whether the validity of political concepts is
indeed entirely relative to historical circumstances and historical traditions. It might be objected that Oakeshott's own principle of genuine love
for human beings embodies an enduring attitude whose essence is unalter-
ed by the vicissitudes of circumstances, though its expressions may vary
under different conditions. The same would apply to the principle of
freedom. Throughout the historical changes undergone by this principle
or rather by its realizations, two elements of its content remain constant. In the first place, it always embodies a value. In other words, in
every political ideology freedom occupies the status of an ideal which
must be perpetuated. In the second place, it is a principle which allows
for a wide range of human activities, on the assumption that man is
endowed with a variety of abilities all of which ought to find actual
expression. It is true that principles of this kind undergo changes of
content in the course of historical development. Thus, for example,
whether or not freedom of property is as essential to human existence
as freedom of faith and speech, has become a moot point. But the very
value of life's various and heterogeneous aspects remains a constant
element of the freedom-principle. An awareness of the constant and,
as it were, phenomenological aspects of freedom is an awareness that
historicist relativism can be confuted.

(4) It is not mere skepticism, but what might be called "expansive"
skepticism which renders Oakeshott's position vulnerable. There would
be no reason for objecting to his skepticism, were it confined to the
possibility of realizing political ideals. Yet he expands his skepticism

---

[42] "The Political Economy of Freedom", *Rationalism in Politics*, p. 40.
[43] "Introduction" to *The Social and Political Doctrines of Contemporary Europe*, p.XXII.
[44] *Ibid.*

to encompass the very need to realize ideals. His premise that the realization of ideals is difficult and creates as many problems as it solves, is sound. But his skeptical conclusion that there is consequently no ideal to be realized, is not.

(5) To conclude our criticism of Oakeshott's general assumptions, it might be permissible to make a somewhat metaphysical observation. According to him, one task of political philosophy is to circumscribe the position of politics within the compass of human existence and experience. The task is formulated in his *Political Education* and executed in his Introduction to *Hobbes' Leviathan*. This seems to imply (a) that Oakeshott does not regard politics as a purely technical matter and (b) that he is accordingly obliged to consider the relation between politics and man's place in the universe.

Man's mastery of his given circumstances, a mastery controlled by principles, pertains to the essence of his place in the universe. Man is never totally submerged in his given circumstances, be those circumstances natural or be they historical. It is by elevating himself above nature and history that man participates in them. And it is by participating in his given circumstances that he masters them. What Oakeshott fails to come to grips with is the issue whether man is exhausted in the circumstances of his existence. Were he aware of man's cosmic status, Oakeshott would not tend to make man a function of his circumstances. Just as Marx made man a function of his social circumstances, so Oakeshott makes man a function of his historical circumstances as embodied in tradition – and this is a strange affinity. And there is as little justification for Marx's brand of historicism as there is for Oakeshott's.

CHAPTER IV

THE HISTORICAL PROCESS AND ITS EXPLANATION: KARL POPPER AND HIS DEBTORS

I.

A schematic classification of different directions of philosophies of history could point out that "classical "philosophical views are concerned with the nature of the historical processes, its components, its meaning, and its goal. In the classical approach, historical understanding is related to an assessment of the historical process. The philosophical problem of history is twofold; both aspects of the problem emerge also in Hegel's discussion of the two sides of the term "history" as the course of events and as its understanding. The classical tradition, in this sense, refers to Hegel, Marx, Comte, Croce, Bradley, etc. who shaped its image. Measured by the general trend of the classical tradition, the more recent interest in history seems to take a different direction which might be characterized, loosely, as methodological.

The new developments in philosophy, occasionally described – not without exaggeration – as a revolution, find their reflection in some approaches to the philosophical problem of history. To generalize, the change in historical theory can be characterized as a shift in orientation from "history" *qua* process and understanding of the process, to "history" *qua* science, knowledge, understanding, general or particular modes of explanation and exposition, and so on. The swing towards a more restrictive methodological orientation is reflected in the tendency to stress the methods of historical explanation. By contrast with the classical approach, which is characterized by a structured relation between history viewed *a parte objecti* and history viewed *a parte subjecti*, the recent approach we are about to consider tends to view the historical process mainly, if not entirely, *a parte subjecti*. This shift in emphasis is translated into an almost exclusive concern with historical explanation or with the historical narrative. Largely influential for this shift are the writings of Carl G. Hempel and William Dray in particular, and the trend towards positivism in general.[1]

This shift is not unambiguous; it is not always easy to determine, when reading recent discussions of historical explanation, whether the writer is concerned with certain aspects of the historical process which dictate certain features of historical explanation, or whether he has offered a methodological analysis of historical explanation proper which he apparently represents as a mode of explanation, controlled by some immanent methodological standard. Before turning to an examination of this ambiguity, as it appears in the writings of K. R. Popper and his debtors, it should perhaps be observed in advance that Popper's vacillation represents only one instance of a more general tendency.

Indeed, not only his approach turns out to be less radically "new" than his avowed orientation to the logic of historical research seems to imply. For all their emphasis upon the methodological aspects of historical explanation, English philosophers do not neglect or ignore the doctrines of their predecessors. In their writings, one finds a positive attitude towards both Collingwood and Oakeshott, an attitude expressed either through acceptance, or through critical evaluation of their teachings.[2] Thus, for example, in his recent re-statement of the nature of scientific explanation – to take a view expressed outside the geographical boundaries of English philosophy – Hempel[3] invokes Collingwood's thesis that to explain a particular historical action is to show that the action "makes sense" to the agent, that it is clear to his reason. Generally speaking, then, philosophizing is less uprooted than it appears, or purports, to be.

With this one reservation granted, the fact remains, however, that there has been a swing towards a restrictive preoccupation with the nature of historical explanation. It is against the background of this shift that we propose to consider Popper's view.

2.

To begin with, it is noteworthy that Popper does not neglect the objective character of the historical process. His concern with this aspect

---

[1] Cf., respectively, "The Function of General Laws in History", *Readings in Philosophical Analysis*, edited by H. Feigl and W. Sellars, New York, 1948, pp. 459–471, and *Laws and Explanation in History*, Oxford, 1957.

[2] On Collingwood see Patrick Gardiner, *The Nature of Historical Explanation*, London, 1952, pp. 46, 47, 77, 115; Oakeshott is discussed on pp. 29–32, 35, 80. On Collingwood see also W. B. Gallie, *Philosophy and the Historical Understanding*, London 1964, pp. 17, 18,46.

[3] C. G. Hempel, "Scientific Explanation", *Voice of America Forum Lectures, Philosophy of Science Series, No. 11*, p. 7.

of history is reflected in his criticism of the view – which Popper correlates with what he calls "historicism" – that human beings are "swept into the future by irresistible forces."[4] Why does Popper disapprove of the view which characterizes the historical process as sustained by irresistible forces? Popper's theory of historical explanation and understanding cannot be reconciled with a totalistic-holistic conception of the historical according to which any partial change or any partial intervention in the course of the process is rendered immutable by the totality of the process. According to Popper, this holistic-deterministic conception of the process is a form of "essentialism," i.e. of a methodological approach, which he describes as an outlook wherein the nature of the global reality converges with the trend of the method of approaching its constituent parts. "Essentialists," Popper writes, "deny that we first count a group of single things and then label them ... 'white'; rather, they say, we call each single white thing 'white' on account of a certain intrinsic property that it shares with other white things, 'whiteness.'"[5] And he adds in the same vein: "The school of thinkers whom I propose to call *methodological essentialists* was founded by Aristotle, who taught that scientific research must penetrate to the essence of things in order to explain them."[6] Popper seems to think that an essentialist approach to history entails the assumption of history's total essence. His presentation of historical essentialism can be summarized as follows: as a total essence, history contains its direction within itself. In virtue of its immanent self-direction, history is a self-regulating totality which absorbs the entire historical process whereby men are swept along inexorably.

To this totalistic or essentialistic view of history, Popper objects on moral, as well as on methodological grounds. The former objection implicitly outlines the negative moral consequences of essentialism. The latter objection explicitly dismisses as misleading the essentialistic question, *What is the historical process?*, and proposes as the only valid question, *How do events occur?*[7] Popper's moral argument against the holistic-essentialistic conception of history is hinted at in the dedication of *The Poverty of Historicism*. The dedication speaks for itself:

---

[4] Karl R. Popper, *The Poverty of Historicism*, London, 1961, p. 160. "Historism" or "Historicism" is an ambiguous term. It is clear that Popper's understanding of the concept is based on a selection of one possible connotation of it. As to the various meanings, consult Karl Heussi, *Die Krisis des Historismus*, Tübingen, 1932.

[5] Popper, *ibid.*, pp. 27–28.

[6] *Ibid.*, p. 28.

[7] *Ibid.*, p. 29.

In memory of the countless men and women
of all creeds or nations or races
who fell victims to the fascist and communist belief in
Inexorable Laws of Historical Destiny.

Popper does not develop this moral argument in the *Poverty of Historicism*, which is devoted to his methodological-epistemological objection against historicism. But the moral and ideological implications of Popper's criticism are thrown into relief by the relation, established in the dedication, between philosophy of history and ideology.

As further evidence of Popper's moral-ideological argument against historicism one can cite the concluding sentences of *The Poverty of Historicism*.

May it not, after all, be the historicists who are afraid of change? And is it not, perhaps, this fear of change which makes them so utterly incapable of reacting rationally to criticism, and which makes others so responsive to their teaching? It almost looks as if historicists were trying to compensate themselves for the loss of an unchanging world by clinging to the faith that change can be foreseen because it is ruled by an unchanging law.[8]

Moral disapproval of historicism is clearly implicit in Popper's suggestion that the view may be the product of fear; for to ascribe to fear the adoption of a particular view is to question the intellectual integrity of its proponent. A note of moral disapproval is also audible in the suggestion that historicism cannot bear the brunt of rational criticism because it lacks a foundation in reason. Compressed in the passage just quoted is the argument that historicism uses essentialism as its philosophical anchor only in order to transform it into ideology. And an ideology – so Popper seems to assume – is by definition a self-contained dogma, beyond the reach of rational criticism, the irrational or anti-rational nature of which is the secret of its appeal to its proponents. Popper's use of the terms "faith" in the characterization of his target leaves no doubt in the reader's mind as to the accusation of irrationalism implicit in the methodological-epistemological criticism.

It should perhaps be pointed out that the partly moral motivation links Popper with the "classical" tradition. As we have suggested, "classical" views are characterized by an intimate interrelation between the objective historical process and the explanation of that process. We may now add that classical views are also characterized by their concern with the moral meaning of the historical process, i.e. with its tendency towards progress or decline, towards rationality or towards mutability, and so on. A similar concern is manifest in Popper's

[8] *Ibid.*, p. 161.

argument that beneath the mask of rationality which historicism dons in parading as a theory of the reason by which history is governed, there lurks an anti-rational attitude and an anti-rational motivation. The spirit of classicism pervades Popper's recurrent assertions that totality, as such, is irrational and that the piecemeal alone can be represented as rational. Armed with this standard of rationality, Popper sets out to elaborate a different approach to the nature of historical understanding.

The problem, according to Popper, is not merely one of "methodological nominalism," or of describing how things behave;[9] it is also one of determining the proper task of history, when history is understood as a human concern by virtue of its goals and explanatory methods alike. History, as Popper puts it, "is interested not only in the explanation of the specific events but also in the description of a specific event."[10] Here history means the understanding of history, i.e. *historia rerum gestarum*. Popper rightly presents the narration of events as fulfilling the twofold task of explaining past events and of describing them. Further Popper adds that "these two tasks of history, the disentanglement of causal threads and the description of the 'accidental' manner in which these threads are interwoven, are both necessary, and they supplement each other; at one time an event may be considered as typical, i.e. from the standpoint of its causal explanation, and at another time as unique."[11] On the one hand, this statement is clearly made *a parte objecti*, i.e. from the viewpoint of events as explained and described. Thus we are told that events may be regarded from different points of view; that they may be considered either as "typical" or as "unique". But on the other hand, the same statement might have been made *a parte subjecti*: for the fact that typical and unique are "interwoven" can be approached from the position of the historical narrative which describes and explains them.

Further evidence of a tension between the position of the explained-and-described state of affairs and the opposition of their explanation-and-description in Popper's approach, is afforded by what Popper stresses as the "most important features" of society: *"its division into periods, and the emergence of novelty."*[12] Perhaps the division into periods may be represented, without reservations, as an explanatory device, or as a means of describing the historical sequence. But from what

[9] Cf. *ibid.*
[10] *Ibid.*, p. 146.
[11] *Ibid.*, p. 147.
[12] *Ibid.*, p. 11.

position are we to regard novelty? Novelty pertains to the emergence from something already in existence of some other thing which does not necessarily follow it. Novelty is an aspect of the process as well as an aspect of the description-and-explanation of what is undergoing the process. One may even say that if novelty constitutes a facet in explanation, it is because novelty constitutes a feature of the state of affairs at which the process has arrived. Thus Popper's description of the twofold task of history does not represent an unambiguous shift towards a methodological consideration of history. In Popper's theory, as in the "classical" views examined earlier, history embraces and interlaces an objective state of affairs and an explanatory-descriptive understanding thereof.

Popper's unacknowledged debt to the classical tradition and the consequent ambiguity of his approach, can be detected in yet other elements of his thought. Consider, for example, the problem of historical prediction which Popper discusses at the beginning of *The Poverty of Historicism*.[13] On the one hand, prediction as asserted or formulated forecast is clearly situated on the plane of history *qua* understanding, knowledge, explanation and description. On the other hand, however, the possibility or impossibility of historical prediction presents a problem which cannot be explored without establishing whether the nature of events allows for prediction or not. That Popper is aware of the interrelation between the two planes seems to be suggested by the following observation:

The idea that a prediction may have an influence upon the predicted event is a very old one. Oedipus ... killed his father ... and this was a direct result of the prophecy which caused his father to abandon him. This is why I suggest the name *"Oedipus effect"* for the influence of the prediction upon the predicted event (or more generally, for the influence of an item of information upon the situation to which the information refers), whether this influence tends to bring about the predicted event, or whether it tends to prevent it.[14]

Popper's distinction between information and situation in this passage, is not as sharp as it appears at first glance. By substituting "state of affairs" or "process" for "situation," we could obtain an *a parte objecti*-approach to history; and by substituting "description" for "information" we could obtain an *a parte subjecti*-approach. The main thing emphasized in this passage is not the distinction between the two aspects of history, but their interrelatedness. Popper's argument is, first, that history *a parte subjecti* influences history *a parte objecti;* and

[13] See *ibid.*, p. 14.
[14] *Ibid.*, p. 13.

secondly, that this influence precludes the possibility of prediction. By interfering in the process to which historical explanation refers, prediction formulated renders the materialization of prediction impossible. While the limits of explanation are circumscribed on the plane of explanation, the limiting factor transcends the plane of explanation proper.

A similar element of ambiguity is discernible in Popper's argument against reasoning from the existence of trends or tendencies, to the operation of laws:

> ... the existence of trends or tendencies in social change can hardly be questioned: every statistician can calculate such trends. Are these trends not comparable with Newton's law of inertia? The answer is: trends exist, or more precisely, the assumption of trends is often a useful statistical device. *But trends are not laws* ...[15]

Popper then proceeds to point out that laws are universal statements which do not assert existence, whereas "a statement asserting the existence of a trend is existential, not universal."[16] The definition of laws here proposed is puzzling. From a Kantian viewpoint, it may be interpreted as meaning that laws are assertions about relations which perception imposes upon given data. This would permit us to place laws on the plane of explanation – to use the terms of the present discussion, or, to use Kantian terms – on the plane of apperception, its categories, and the statements based upon them. But on what plane are we to place "trends?" Popper himself speaks of them now as existing facets of the historical process, now as "statistical devices," that is, now as pertaining to history *a parte objecti*, now as pertaining to history *a parte subjecti*.

As in the case of historical prediction, so in the case of trends – albeit to a less marked degree – the two aspects of history are interwoven in Popper. Nor is the analogy between the two cases coincidental. Towards the end of the passage considered above, Popper correlates his discussion of laws and trends with the earlier discussion of historical prediction in the following manner:

> ... a statement asserting the existence of a trend at a certain time and place would be a singular historical statement, not a universal law. The practical significance of this logical situation is considerable: while we may base scientific predictions on laws, we cannot (as every cautious statistician knows) base them merely on the existence of trends. A trend (we may ... take population growth as an example) which has persisted for hundreds or even thousands of years may change within a decade, or even more rapidly than that.[17]

[15] *Ibid.*, p. 115.
[16] *Ibid.*
[17] *Ibid.*

And he continues in the same vein when he observes that "explained trends do exist, but their persistence depends on the persistence of certain specific initial conditions."[18]

What motivates Popper to take an ambiguous position that cannot be confined within the limits of historical explanation? Why does he occasionally swing back from the plane of explanation to the plane of the process? In the discussion of historical prediction, interference or intervention accounts for the shift. For to intervene in a process is possible only on the plane of the process – even when the impetus towards intervention comes from prediction, i.e. from what may be regarded as an explanatory attitude. This element of intervention recurs in Popper's discussion of "Piecemeal *versus* Utopian Engineering."[19] Using the term "Social engineering" to denote "social activities ... which, in order to realize some aim or end, consciously utilize all available technological knowledge,"[20] Popper distinguishes between "Holistic or Utopian social engineering," of which he disapproves, and "piecemeal engineering" which he advocates:

> The piecemeal technologist or engineer recognizes that *only a minority of social institutions are consciously designed while the vast majority have just "grown," as the undesigned results of human actions* ... Holistic or Utopian social engineering, as opposed to piecemeal social engineering, is never of a "private" but always of a "public" character. It aims at remodelling the "whole of society" in accordance with a definite plan or blueprint. ... [21]

The objections against holisitic engineering are based upon his general thesis that it is impossible to embrace the historical process in its totality. To address himself to the historical process, an agent must isolate certain fragments or regions thereof. These may be, or are, regarded as amenable to alteration through intervention either in the course of events, or in the course of institutional action. However, any form of engineering, holistic or piecemeal, represents a mode of action carried out by human agents within the process. Neither the engineering attitude nor the engineering action are adopted and sustained from the position of explanation; both require that we adopt a position within, and in relation to, the process.

A similar distinction is drawn by Popper between holistic and piece-

---

[18] *Ibid.*, p. 128.
[19] *Ibid.*, p. 65.
[20] *Ibid.*
[21] *Ibid.*, pp. 65, 67.

meal historical narration. Even as engineering is possible only in relation to selected regions of the process, history

... can only deal with selected aspects of the object in which it is interested. It is a mistake to believe that there can be a history in the holistic sense, a history of "States of Society" which represent "the whole of the social organism" or "all the social and historical events of an epoch." This idea derives from an intuitive view of a *history of mankind* as a vast and comprehensive stream of development. But such a history cannot be written. Every written history is a history of a certain narrow aspect of this "total" development, and is anyhow a very incomplete history even of the particular incomplete aspect chosen.[22]

The selective character of *written* history corresponds to the piecemeal character of engineering in what might be called *executed* history. Popper denies the possibility of holism both on the plane of the process and on the plane of description-and-explanation, but at the same time a distinction should be drawn between written history and executed history. Written history, as written, calls for various explanatory and descriptive devices which can be employed only from a position of detachment from the process explained and described. Executed history, by contrast, does not always call for deliberate action on the part of the intervening human agent or agents.

There is thus abundant evidence that Popper is concerned both with history as process and with history as description and explanation. At times the two aspects of history coincide, as in the discussion of prediction; at times the two aspects are parallel, as in the discussion of social engineering and historical writing. An element of ambiguity is introduced by Popper's vacillation between emphasis upon the descriptive-explanatory aspect, and occasional recourse to the ontological aspect. This vacillation derives from the consideration of the historical process as furnishing the factual grounds upon which the possibility and the limits of explanation depend.

Perhaps the most crucial coincidence of history as process and history as explanation occurs in Popper's conception of "situation logic" or the "logic of the situation."[23] Arguing that "there is room for a more detailed analysis of *the logic of situations*," Popper maintains that "the best historians have often made us, more or less unconsciously, aware of this conception: Tolstoy, for example, when he describes how it was not decision but "necessity" which made the Russian army yield Moscow without a fight and withdraw to places where it could find food,..."[24]

[22] *Ibid.*, pp. 80–81.
[23] See *ibid.*, p. 147.
[24] *Ibid.*, p. 149.

Audible in the term "situational logic" is an echo of the term *"Sachverhalt"* which, in phenomenological literature is used to denote the investigated state of affairs. By a state of affairs, the phenomenologist means a plane of things or facts which lie beyond the sphere of mere propositions, i.e. beyond the sphere which in Phenomenology constitutes the topic formulated in the logic of statements or, to use Husserl's term, *"apophantics."*Closely related to the "state of affairs" of Phenomenology, is the "situation" of Existentialism. The trans-propositional sphere denoted by the term "situation" lends itself to various specifications. In certain discussions, "situation" means the structure of the political field which determines the nature of a particular action.[25] In Popper's writings, "situation" means a fragment of the historical process, a state of affairs within the process. By "situational logic" Popper apparently means the conclusions which men draw from a particular situation encountered by them or surrounding them. Like the facets of Popper's thought examined above, this concept of situational logic is ambiguous. At times it seems to connote those factors in a given situation which prompt men to adopt a particular course of action; at times – as in Tolstoy's account of the Russian surrender – it seems to connote an observer's explanation of men's action in response to a given situation; and finally, it connotes both the response and its explanation. Seen through the ambiguities examined above, the ambiguity of "situational logic" does not seem to be incidental. Like the ambiguity of prediction, trends, engineering, and writing of history it reflects the "classical" duality of Popper's entire theory.

3.

Popper's influence upon other philosophers who have elaborated a theory of explanation in history is openly acknowledged by his debtors. A typical case in point is the following passage from Patrick Gardiner's book on *The Nature of Historical Explanation:*

History is primarily concerned with human beings and what they have done. When the historian comes to ask why they did what they did, he sometimes answers by referring to general laws of human response to specified types of situation; and sometimes by referring to what Professor Popper has called "the logic of the situation," i.e. in terms of what it would be reasonable to do in such-and-such circumstances, and with such-and-such objectives in view.[26]

Like Popper, then, Gardiner maintains that an historical explanation

---

[25] Here lies also the origin of the ethico-theological concept, *"Situationsethik"*.
[26] P. Gardiner, *The Nature of Historical Explanation*, London 1952, p. 49.

can be given either by tracing the typical pattern illustrated by the particular action explained, or by characterizing the specific complexity of the situation here-and-now. But whereas in Popper's presentation the emphasis is upon the sustained tension between typical and unique, in Gardiner's presentation stronger stress is laid upon the typical. Gardiner maintains that,

we need no longer take seriously the view that, since the historian is interested in unique events, his subject-matter is, *on these grounds*, incapable of being generalized about ... The engineer is concerned with building particular bridges. The architect is concerned with designing particular houses. Like the engineer and the architect, the historian is concerned with reconstructing particular situations in the past. But, just as neither the architect nor the engineer is free to ignore the laws of mechanics in his work, so ... the historian, for all his attention to the individual and the unique, is not free to disregard general laws in his work of reconstruction.[27]

Gardiner does not claim that historical generalizations have the same validity as the laws of mechanics. To speak in Kantian terms, he conceives of their function as regulative, not as constituting. Discussing the distinction between the scientist and the historian, Gardiner writes:

The scientist frames hypotheses of precision and wide generality by a continual refining away of irrelevant factors. Things are otherwise with the historian. His aim is to talk about what happened on particular occasions in all its variety, all its richness, and his terminology is adapted to this object. That is the reason why terms like "revolution" are left so vague and so open. They are accommodating terms ... Generalizations about revolutions, class-struggles, civilizations, must *inevitably* be vague, open to a multitude of exceptions ... because of the looseness of the terms they employ ... But this is not to criticize such generalizations provided that they are not expected to do more work than they are fitted for. The scientific model of precise correlation is misleading in any attempt to comprehend the role of these generalizations in history, where they function frequently as *guides to understanding*.[28]

On the basis of this passage alone, there is no warrant for concluding that Gardiner is concerned with the nature of historical understanding, that he takes his departure from the task of the historian, and that he characterizes historical understanding in terms of the devices instrumental in carrying out this task. In his treatment of the immanent problem presented by historical explanation, Gardiner tends to lay less stress on the regulative role of the situation, which calls for the adoption of pertinent devices, than on the devices adopted and their hypothetical nature. Gardiner's tendency to emphasize the perspective or standpoint of explanation finds clear expression in the concluding paragraphs of

[27] *Ibid.*, p. 45.
[28] *Ibid.*

The Nature of Historical Explanation. Taking exception to "the apparent antinomy (which) arises out of the view that the world is made up, on the one hand, of "dead matter", and, on the other, of mind," Gardiner observes that:

> Whether we regard human beings in their "physical" aspects or in their "mental" aspects depends upon our interests. . . . There is no conflict, only a difference of point of view and purpose. . . . Human beings are not "really matter" or "really mind": they are human beings. Different ways of talking about them, dictated by different interests, have been hypostatized into different ingredients.[29]

The burden of Gardiner's argument is a variation on the distinction between material language and formal language. Gardiner evidently favours the notion of formal language and the theory that the various modes of expression included in the realm of formal language are determined by various interests and purposes. Conspicuous by its absence from his analysis of historical explanation is an account of the relation between a particular situation and the specific way of talking about it adopted by the historian. Here explanation is represented as autonomous; the "interests" referred to are embraced by the explanation and not by the situation. The various possible modes of explanation are treated with tolerance, and their adoption or rejection is represented as a matter of methodological decision:

> We do explain human actions in terms of reaction to environment. But we also explain human actions in terms of thoughts, desires, and plans. We may believe that it is in principle possible to give full causal explanation of why people think, desire, or plan the things they do in terms of their past experience or training, or perhaps in terms of the workings of their bodies. But, even if the latter proposition is true, it still does not follow that explanation in terms of thoughts and desires has been rendered superfluous, or that it has been 'reduced' to cause-effect explanation. Nor does it follow that human action is never 'free' or 'rational'. The rules for the use of these words are not governed by considerations regarding the possibility of giving a causal explanation.[30]

The methodological-formal bias of Gardiner's view, which is brought into sharp relief by the last sentence of that passage, is prominent but not exclusive. For in dealing with human beings, Gardiner shifts over – in the very passages we quoted above – from formal to material language. He talks about what human beings *are*, as well as about how human beings are *looked at* in different ways dictated by different interests. "Human beings," he asserts, "are not 'really matter' or 'really mind'; they are human beings."[31] The methodological distinction be-

[29] *Ibid.*, pp. 138–139.
[30] *Ibid.*, p. 139.
[31] *Ibid.*

tween formal and material language must be recognized as methodological only. Care must be taken not to represent a way of talking as an element of the situation talked about. It is a mistake to hypostatize a way of talking by projecting it into a state of affairs. Care must also be taken not to reduce human beings to the particular aspect isolated by a particular way of talking about them. Human beings are engaged in material situations; human nature is more comprehensive and more complex than any explanation can possibly suggest. By ignoring the methodological-selective character of the explanation, Gardiner argues, and by projecting the restrictive explanation onto the explained situation philosophers produce "monistic theories of historical explanation."[32] Mistaking explanation for situation, they formulate doctrines which place exclusive emphasis either on the causal nature of the process or on the unique nature of situations. Thus Gardiner's view goes beyond its own methodological bias. In themselves, the methodological considerations which it elaborates are controlled by a non-methodological yardstick. Above and beyond the immanent methodological measures of "interest" and "purpose" is another standard by which explanations are evaluated: the twofold standard implicit in (a) the comprehensive nature of human beings and in (b) the complex nature of the situations in which human beings are engaged. Having shifted over towards methodology, Gardiner cannot do without a common-sense anthropology and a presupposed, non-methodological, understanding of the process.

The complexity of historical situations, which cannot be exhausted by any methodological explanation, is discussed by Gardiner in relation to "the problem of historical connexions." To summarize his thesis that there can be no simple account of historical connexion, Gardiner writes:

Historical situations present a multitude of interrelated factors whose relevance or irrelevance to the events we wish to explain is difficult to determine. The more complex the events dealt with, the wider their spread in time and space, the greater are the calls made upon the historian's judgment.[33]

What Gardiner seems to assume, here, is a knowledge-within-knowledge, a pre-methodological grasp of the given historical situation in its intricately wrought texture, a pre-existing perception presupposed by, and implicit in, our knowledge that the given situation is a complex one. He also seems to assume that our methodological knowledge is deter-

[32] Ibid.
[33] Ibid., p. 98.

mined – to a certain extent – by this implicit, pre-methodological, pre-existing knowledge. Methodological explanations are regulated not only by "interest" and "purpose" but also by an understanding of history which is not exhausted in any explanation of history. Needless to say, these assumptions undercut or counteract the programmatic tendency towards confining "history" within the sphere of its descriptive-explanatory aspect.

The necessary failure of the exclusive methodological approach in disregarding the objective aspect of history finds further reflection in Gardiner's observations concerning the explanation of unique events. On one occasion he describes such explanations by way of analogy with military and political stratagems. "The historian," he writes, "like the general or the statesman, tends to *assess* rather than to *conclude*."[34] Gardiner does not pursue the analogy; but it seems safe to conclude that like the general and the statesman, the historian deals with specific, circumscribed, unique situations not by drawing final conclusions from them, but by appraising their given character. That by "assessment" Gardiner means "description," seems to follow from what he says elsewhere with regard to the task of the historian. According to Gardiner, "the historian tells a story. He is engaged upon describing what happened at a particular time and place and in what particular circumstances...."[35] Here again, the explanation is regulated by the extra-methodological nature of the situation.

That description cannot be confined to the explanatory-methodological plane of history, is witnessed by the theory of Gallie, who – like Gardiner – acknowledges his debt to Popper openly. Like Gardiner, Gallie invokes Popper's concept of situational logic.[36] But Gallie moves even farther away than Gardiner from Popper's broad, dual approach and the tension sustained therein between *res gestae* and *historia rerum gestarum*. In the view we are about to consider, the realm of *historia rerum gestarum* is represented as almost completely self-enclosed. Nevertheless, within the limits of this domain, historical narrative is characterized by the same features which in Popper's broader view are represented as characterizing the realm of history. Gallie's entire analysis is designed to transfer the distinguishing marks of the objective situation dealt with by the historical narrative, to the immanent sphere of historical narration proper. This design is thrown into prominent relief by "the emphasis ... put on the idea of narrative."[37] The novelty of

[34] *Ibid.*, p. 95.
[35] *Ibid.*, p. 82.
[36] Gallie, W. Z. *Philosophy and the Historical Understanding*, New York, 1964, pp. 118–119.
[37] *Ibid.*, p. 9.

this shift in emphasis is rendered explicit. "I find it astonishing," Gallie writes, "that no critical philosopher of history has as yet offered us a clear account of what it is to follow, or to construct an historical narrative ... The effects of this ommision are as great as those that we might expect if in philosophies of science we were to find no discussion of the measurement or of controlled observation."[38]

While it cannot be claimed, without exaggeration, that no philosopher of history considered the character of historical narrative, Gallie's argument can be accepted in a more moderate form. In the classical tradition the narration, or story, or description is represented as intimately interrelated with the objective aspect of history as process. With due allowance for the ambiguity of his position, even Popper still sustains this interrelation. Gallie divorces the aspect of narrative from the aspect of process. But, as we have hinted, features hitherto represented as characterizing the process, are now represented by Gallie as characterizing the narrative.

Thus, for example, answering the question, "What is a story?" Gallie writes:

Every story describes a sequence of actions and experiences of a number of people, real or imaginary. These people are usually presented in some characteristic human situation, and are then shown either changing it or reacting to changes which affect the situation from the outside ... following a story is, at one level, a matter of understanding words. ... But at a much more important level, it means to understand the successive actions and thoughts and feelings of certain described characters with a peculiar directness, and to be pulled forward by this development almost against our will. ...[39]

While at first glance this passage might seem to contain a purely formal analysis of the story as story, upon closer consideration it turns out to have touched inadvertently upon the subject-matter. Even if it is granted that the subject-matter is dealt with on the plane of the story alone, one can still ask: Why is the story about people? How do we know that the story describes a sequence of actions and experiences? Why is it that the story not only relates the impressions made by events on people, but also explains the actions carried out by people in response to changing events? Does not the concern with human beings, or with human actions, or with both men and their actions, constitute the *differentia specifica* of history? Does the conception of sequence dawn upon us like a *Deus ex machina?* Does it not rather presuppose the concept of time? Is time only a coordinate of the story? Is it not, moreover, a coordinate of events and actions as well?

[38] *Ibid.*, p. 13.
[39] *Ibid.*, p. 22.

Paradoxically enough, we are forced to transcend formalism even by the formalistic assertion that at one level, understanding a story is "a matter of understanding words, sentences, paragraphs, set out in order." Obviously one cannot understand an historical narrative unless one understands the words in which it is communicated. But what does understanding words mean? Does not the verbal medium point beyond itself to the trans-linguistic features of "successive actions and feelings?" May we accordingly regard as merely a didactic device the stress laid by Gallie on the aspect of the story, the emphasis which is so strong that it represents the story as the exclusive concern of "a critical philosophy of history?" Yet even a purely formal analysis of the story inevitably leads to whatever it is that the story is about. The conclusion may be trivial; but the triviality cannot be overcome by any methodological analysis.

Further evidence that Gallie cannot do without the objective aspect of history is furnished by his consideration of the element of contingency in the story. To understand his argument, it is helpful to recall that according to Popper, the interweaving of the typical and the unique in the process must be accounted for by the explanation. Translating this point in terms of his own theory, Gallie ascribes to the "story" the two aspects which Popper ascribes to the process and its explanation:

Why are certain contingencies acceptable in relation to the story whereas others are not? ... A story is understood or followed on the basis of (a) certain general traits that are ascribed to its characters, settings etc., and (b) certain chances or contingencies that befall its characters. These latter help to shape the story's development in one particular way; but other contingencies, or combinations of contingencies ... would have made – not a story at all, but a sequence of accidents that led us nowhere, that added up to nothing, that signified or told us nothing. Hence the question, "What makes certain contingencies acceptable in a particular story?" is virtually equivalent to the question, "What makes a particular story followable?" and is best answered by an analysis of what it means to follow a story.[40]

Judging from this passage, we may conclude that Gallie is concerned with the acceptability of the story, not with the nature of the process. In view of his allusion to "what makes a particular story followable" and in view of his earlier association of acceptability with "intelligibility"[41] Gallie is apparently concerned with the reader's judgment of the story. As a result of the transfer from process to story, the measure

---

[40] *Ibid.*, p. 33. Professor E. Gellner observes on this issue "Gallie is not merely a philosopher concerned with contingency, he has something like a passion for it". See his "The Concept of Story", *Ratio*, Vol. IX, June 1967, pp. 49ff.
[41] *Ibid.*, p. 27.

of the story is no longer adequacy but intelligibility; and the test of intelligibility is the judgment of the potential listener or reader. Needless to say, the historian may be his own audience, as a poet may sing to himself.

On the plane of the story, that which was typical on the plane of the process becomes "certain general traits"; and that which was unique on the plane of the process, becomes "certain chances or contingencies." The story may become more interesting through the interplay of general trait with particular contingency; but it cannot thereby become true. This is the price a story must pay for its emancipation. If the world of the story is self-contained, confined within its own immanent limits, and referring to nothing beyond them, then Gallie can maintain that "ideally, a story should be self-explanatory."[42] Ideally, in other words, to be an immanent entity is to be self-explanatory. But it is we who create the self-contained world of the story; it is to us that it owes its self-explanatory immanence. It is we who project onto the plane of the story, in the form of general traits and particular contingencies, the features of the process to which it corresponds; and it is owing to this projection that it is now immanent.

According to Gallie, "the primary task of history, distinguishing it from all forms of scientific thought, is to display ... contingent happenings in their mutual intrusiveness."[43] On what grounds does Gallie assign history the task of displaying contingencies in their mutual intrusiveness? Would he agree with Gardiner that it is purely a matter of "interest," "purpose," and "point of view?" Or would he admit that it is also a matter of, so to speak, the "situational logic" of the historical concern in general? If he would make the latter admission, then he would also have to admit that it is impossible to divorce the historical concern from the objective situation to which the story is related. To argue otherwise, is to echo the positivistic emphasis on language as a self-contained sphere.

As we have already noticed, a tendency towards a positivistic emphasis on language is discernible in Gallie's argument that "following a story is, at one level, a matter of understanding words, sentences, paragraphs, set out in order." It may now be added that the same tendency finds further reflection in Gallie's claim that historical "understanding, ... with its obvious affinities to artistic appreciation, is something very different from explanation in the theoretical or

---

[42] *Ibid.*, p. 23.
[43] *Ibid.*, p. 14.

scientific sense."[44] In Gallie's terms, one could say that this assertion is self-explanatory because it is consistent with his theory as a whole.

Gallie makes another isomorphic projection of material language onto story-language in his discussion of prediction. The problem of prediction is connected with the assumption that to be acceptable, a story must be intelligible. As associated with this immanent characteristic of the story, predictability presupposes a relation between the story and the reader, rather than – as in Popper's view – a relation between the explanation and the process. Whereas according to Popper, prediction is characteristic of the explanation which refers to events that take place in the course of a real process, according to Gallie, intelligibility is a characteristic of the story that refers to events which occur within the limits of the story-world. Speaking of the conclusion of the story, Gallie observes that "in the typical case we come to it, wait for it, follow the story through and up to it, it is something unpredictable yet in its own way intelligible and acceptable ...."[45] With due allowance for this difference between the planes on which predictability is considered by Popper and Gallie respectively, one discerns, however, the same interplay between predictable and unpredictable factors in Gallie's analysis of the story as that which characterized Popper's analysis of the relation between process and explanation. The elements of intelligibility and "surprise"[46] in Gallie's analysis correspond respectively to the elements of predictability and unpredictability in Popper's analysis.

The element of surprise or unpredictability is not unintelligible, Gallie maintains. To be accepted by the reader, it too must somehow be pertinent to, or integrated in, the sequence of the story. The role of surprise in Gallie's story resembles the role of *Deus ex machina*. Even as the latter device was acceptable to the audience, so "surprises: ... coincidences, unforeseeable recognitions and revelations, and other fortuituous, happy or unhappy, events," Gallie claims, "should never offend our sense of what is possible, or even acceptable, in the circumstances supposed. Nevertheless, the conclusion of a good story – a conclusion which we wait for eagerly – is not something that could have been or should have been foreseen."[47]

Why does the reader accept "surprises?" Why does he find them intelligible? It seems impossible to answer this question without con-

44 *Ibid.*
45 *Ibid.*, p. 27.
46 *Ibid.*, p. 23.
47 *Ibid.*, p. 24.

sidering prediction in relation to the main characteristic of history as process, not as story; as *res gestae*, not as *historia rerum gestarum*. For what renders surprises intelligible, Gallie admits, is the reader's "dominant sense of alternative possibilities: events in train are felt to admit of different possible outcomes."[48]

What the reader cannot foresee, the element of the conclusion which comes as a surprise to him, is the one particular outcome among the intelligible possibilities which will come true. Thus, "although recognised, this predictable aspect of life is, so to speak, recessive or in shadow. It is in contrast to the generally recognised realm of predictable uniformities that the unpredictable developments of a story stand out, as worth making a story of, and as worth following."[49]

This passage echoes Popper's observation that "while we may base scientific predictions on laws, we cannot ... base laws merely on the existence of trends." Corresponding to Popper's distinction between laws and trends, is Gallie's distinction between following a story to its conclusion and recognizing that the conclusion occurred. Following is a process in which the reader deliberately traces the development of events towards a particular outcome; recognition is the act whereby the reader assesses the actual occurrence of a particular outcome. Banished through the door, the objective characteristics of the historical situation return through the window, on the plane of the story – historical explanation being the window through which *res gestae* are readmitted.

This is not to deny the significant difference between the problem of predictability in Popper's view, and the problem of intelligibility in Gallie's view. As we have seen, Popper's concern with historical explanation referring to historical process, drove him to consider the interplay between the two planes as crystallized in the concept and attitude of prediction. Gallie, by contrast, precludes the possibility of any interplay of explanation and process by laying exclusive stress on the plane of the story. Gallie's approach leaves no room for the element of intervention which, as we have seen, formed the bridge between the two planes of history in Popper's theory. By the very logic of the situation, reducing historical explanation to telling a story prevents the projection onto the story-world of the interplay of process and explanation.

It may not be by chance that Gallie's conception of historical explanation does not involve an attempt to find a place for political philos-

48 *Ibid.*, p. 26.
49 *Ibid.*

ophy within the realm of historical philosophy.[50] The inevitable outcome of divorcing historical explanation from historical process, is the
divorce of theory from practice, of the form of history from its content.
There is one respect in which – for all its protests to the contrary –
traditional English philosophy belongs to the classical tradition of
Greek philosophy, namely its preoccupation with the philosophical
problems of politics. But in some present-day trends, the repudiation
of the classical heritage reaches an extreme; for the first time, the story
signifies nothing – neither process nor politics. Paradoxically enough,
self-explanation becomes as dogmatic as the "dogmatic" philosophies
purportedly abandoned by the new trends in philosophy. For what is
dogmatism, if not making one's own premises, rather than the nature
of things, the ultimate measure?

The real issue at stake here is not confined to the lack of an interest
in philosophical interpretations of problems of politics. Politics is taken
here by way of *pars pro toto*. The question raised might be formulated
as follows: can an interpretation of history be confined to explanation
of historical facts or is it bound to move to a broader assessment of
the sphere of history? Or to put it differently again: can historical explanation disregard the pre-methodical issues, and in the first place
the contours of the historical realm. That realm is characterized by
the fundamental fact that human beings involved in shaping the processes of history are concurrently with that, engaged in an interpretation and exploration of history, in that they compliment that cognitive activity on the level of their day to day existence or else on the
level of a methodical and deliberate enterprise. History, as human
sciences in general, is characterized by an interaction between the
ontological identity between the subject and the object and by the
maximum effort of the subject to approach the realm methodically, in
spite of the identity.

This aspect has to be accounted for and no methodology of historical
research can abstract itself from its background.

---

[50] To be sure, Gallie deals with concepts of politics as historical concepts. Yet because of
his concern with the sphere of "story", he is bound to disregard the aspects of the political
shaping of the historical process. Politics is obviously an activity within the process. Cf. Gellner's article referred to before.

BIBLIOGRAPHY

OF BOOKS AND ARTICLES MENTIONED IN THE TEXT

BERLIN, I., *The Hedgehog and the Fox*, London, Weidenfeld and Nicholson, 1954.
— *Historical Inevitability*, Geoffrey Cumberlege, Oxford University Press, London, 1954. This essay with others is included in: *Four Essays on Liberty*, Oxford University Press, London–Oxford–New York, 1969.
— "History and Theory, The Concept of Scientific History," *History and Theory*, Vol. I, 1960.
— *Two Concepts of Liberty*, Oxford, Clarendon Press, 1958.
CASSIRER, E., *Philosophy of Symbolic Forms*, New Haven, Yale University Press, 1953–1957. (*Philosophie der Symbolischen Formen*, Bruno Cassirer, Berlin, 1923–1929.)
COLLINGWOOD, R. G., *An Autobiography*, Penguin, London, 1944.
— *An Essay on Metaphysics*, Oxford, Clarendon Press, 1940.
— "Croce's Philosophy of History," *The Hibbert Journal*, Vol. XIX.
— *Essay on Philosophical Method*, Oxford, Clarendon Press, 1933.
— *Outlines of a Philosophy of Art*, London, Oxford University Press, 1925.
— *Religion and Philosophy*, London, Macmillan, 1916.
— *Ruskin's Philosophy, An Address*, Titus Wilson & Son, London, 1920.
— "Some Perplexities about Time," *Proceedings of the Aristotelian Society*, Vol. XXVI, London, 1925–1926.
— *Speculum Mentis*, Oxford, Clarendon Press, 1924.
— *The Idea of History*, ed. T. M. Knox, Oxford, Clarendon Press, 1945.
— *The Idea of Nature*, Oxford, Clarendon Press, 1945.
— "The Limits of Historical Knowledge," *Journal of Philosophical Studies*, Vol. 3/10, 1928.
— "The Nature and Aims of a Philosophy of History," *Proceedings of the Aristotelian Society*, Vol. XXV, 1924–1925.
— *The New Leviathan*, Oxford, Clarendon Press, 1942.
D'ENTRÈVES, A. P., *Natural Law, An Introduction to Legal Philosophy*, London, Hutchinson's University Library, 1951.
DRAY, W., *Laws and Explanation in History*, Oxford, Clarendon Press, 1957.
FEIGL, H. and SELLARS, W. (eds.), *Readings in Philosophical Analysis*, New York, Appleton-Century-Crofts, 1948.
GALLIE, W. B., *Philosophy and the Historical Understanding*, London, Chatto & Windus, 1964.
GARDINER, P., *The Nature of Historical Explanation*, London, Oxford University Press, 1952.
GELLNER, E., "The Concept of a Story," *Ratio*, Vol. IX, 1967.
GROLL, M., "On Human Dignity," *Megamot*, Vol. 3, 1951.
HEMPEL, C. G., "Scientific Explanation," *Voice of America Forum Lectures, Philosophy of Science Series*, No. 11.

HEUSSI, K., *Die Krisis des Historismus*, Tübingen, J. C. B. Mohr (Paul Siebeck), 1932.

HOBBES, T., *Leviathan*, ed. M. Oakeshott, Oxford, Blackwell, 1962.

HUSSERL, E., *Philosophie als Strenge Wissenschaft*, transl. as *Philosophy as a Rigorous Science* in *Phenomenology and the Crisis of Philosophy*, tr. and ed. by A. Lauer, New York, Harper and Row, 1965.

KANT, I., *Critique of Pure Reason*, tr. N. Kemp-Smith, London, Macmillan, 1950.

KRAUSZ, M. (ed.), *Critical Essays on the Philosophy of R. G. Collingwood*, Oxford, Clarendon Press, 1972.

MILL, J. S., *Autobiography*, Oxford, World's Classics, 1935.

OAKESHOTT, M., "Contemporary British Politics," *The Cambridge Journal*, Vol. I, 1947–1948.

— *Experience and its Modes*, Cambridge, Cambridge University Press, 1933.

— *Rationalism in Politics and other Essays*, London, Methuen, 1962.

— "Review of J. D. Mabbott's 'The State and the Citizen'," *Mind*, Vol. LVIII, 1949.

— "Science and Society," *The Cambridge Journal*, Vol. I, 1947–1948.

— *The Social and Political Doctrines of Contemporary Europe*, Cambridge University Press, 1941.

— "The Universities," *The Cambridge Journal*, Vol. II, 1948–1949.

POPPER, K. R., *The Open Society and Its Enemies*, 1st ed., London, Routledge, 1945.

— *The Poverty of Historicism*, London, Routledge & Kegan Paul, 1957.

ROTENSTREICH, N., *Between Past and Present, An Essay on History*, Yale University Press, New Haven, Conn., 1958. Reprinted by Kennikat Press Port Washington, New York–London, 1973.

— "Cassirer's Philosophy of Symbolic Forms and the Problem of History," *Theoria*, Vol. XVIII, 1952.

— "On Lévi-Strauss' Concept of Structure," *The Review of Metaphysics*, Vol. XXV, 1972.

— *On the Human Subject, Studies in the Phenomenology of Ethics and Politics*, Springfield, Ill., C.C. Thomas, 1966.

— *Spirit and Man, An Essay on Being and Value*, Martinus Nijhoff, The Hague, 1963.

— *The Recurring Pattern, Studies in Anti-Judaism in Modern Thought*, London, Weidenfeld and Nicholson, Ltd., 1963.

RUBINOFF, L., *Collingwood and the Reform of Metaphysics, A Study in the Philosophy of Mind*, University of Toronto Press, Toronto, 1970.

STRAUSS, L., "On Collingwood's Philosophy of History," *The Review of Metaphysics*, Vol. V/4, 1952.

INDEX OF NAMES

SUBJECT INDEX

abstract, abstractness, 3f., 26
activity, 13f.
action, 35
agent, 93f.
alienation, 102
American Revolution, 84
amor fati, 83
analytic philosophy, 105f.
Anstoss, 52, 57
anticipation, 71, 94f.
a parte objecti, 6, 14, 23, 132, 136, 137f.
a parte subjecti, 6, 12, 14, 15, 23, 38, 132, 136, 137f.
apperception, 38
a priori, 56
a priorism, 85
approval, 15
art, 41f.
assertion, 2f., 26, 41
asylum ignovantiae, 85

"Baconian approach", 12f., 53f.
barbarians, 80, 81, 88, 110
becoming, 80f.
behaviour, 123f.
belief, 54
Biblical history, 59
Bolshevism, 99

categorical imperative, 102
categorical statement, 2f.
causality, 3f., 107, 143
chance, 85
change, 74f., 113f., 135f.
Christianity, 94f.
circumstances, 127f.
civility, 81
civilization, 79f.
classical, 132f.
coherence, 44

common sense, 92, 104f.
Communism, 98
comprehemsivemess, 123f.
concrete, concreteness, 3f., 73
conservatism, 121
"consciousness in general", 77
constitutive, 142
constructions, 2f., 41f.
contemplation, 35
contingencies, 148f.
continuity, 125f.
"Copernican turn", 54, 63, 72
correspondence, 44
criticism, 124f.
"cunning of reason", 12

data, 49f.
decision, 35, 53
deducibility, 2
development, 80
dialectic, 20f., 27f., 29, 46, 49, 52, 59, 60, 86f.
dogmatism, 21, 41, 93f., 119
doubt, 52
duty, 81f., 107

education, 118f.
empirical self, 107
empricism, 105, 118
eristic, 87f.
escapism, 101f.
essentialism, 134f.
eternity, 61
ethics, 105f.
evaluation, 94f.
evidence, 44, 51f.
evil, 93, 95, 128f.
evolution, 77f., 118f.
existentialism, 91, 100, 141
experience, experiencing, 31, 41, 91, 118f.